Vanessa-Ann's

Crafts For Kids

80 Totally Excellent Projects

Vanessa-Ann's

Crafts For Kids

80 Totally Excellent Projects

Meredith® Press

New York, New York

Meredith® Press is an imprint of Meredith® Books:

President, Book Group: Joseph J. Ward
Vice President, Editorial Director:
Elizabeth P. Rice

For Meredith® Press
Executive Editor: Maryanne Bannon
Project Editor: Barbara Tchabovsky
Associate Editor: Guido Anderau
Production Manager: Bill Rose
Jacket Design: Howard Roberts

For Chapelle LTD.

Owners:
Terrece Beesley
Jo Packham

Staff:
Trice Boerens
Tina Annette Brady
Sandra Durbin Chapman
Holly Fuller
Kristi Glissmeyer
Susan Jorgensen
Margaret Shields Marti
Jackie McCowen
Barbara Milburn
Pamela Randall
Jennifer Roberts
Florence Stacey
Lew Stoddard
Nancy Whitley
Gloria Zirkel

Designers:
Terrece Beesley
Trice Boerens
Margaret Shields Marti
Jo Packham
Jennifer Roberts
Florence Stacey

Photographer:
Ryne Hazen

The photographs in this book were taken at the homes of Jody and John Coy, Jo Packham and Penelope Hammond. Other photos were taken at Mary Gaskill's Trends & Traditions, Ogden UT, and The Children's Hour, Salt Lake City, UT. Their cooperation and trust are deeply appreciated.

ISBN: 0-696-02387-3 (Hardcover)
ISBN: 0-696-02498-5 (Trade Paperback)
Library of Congress Catalog Card Number: 92-085219

First Printing 1993

Published by Meredith® Press
Distributed by Meredith® Corporation,
Des Moines IA

10 9 8 7 6 5 4 3 2 1
All rights reserved.
Printed in the United States of America

To Shirley–
*on behalf of all the children
and grandchildren you have loved,
supported and entertained!*
T–

Contents

NOTE: Small sewn-on or glued-on trims, such as buttons or confetti are not safe to use on crafts that will be given to very young children, who might swallow them by mistake. If you plan to give a craft to a child under 4, ask a grown-up if the trims in the check list are safe to use. If they are not, you can paint or draw the trims onto the craft project instead.

Scratched Rainbow Notes

There's nothing more special than a handmade Valentine or note card.
The message seems twice as nice when it's written on something you make yourself.

Ask a grown-up to help you purchase some of the check-list items.

I LOVE YOU

CHECK LIST
❑ 7-inch by 10-inch piece of heavy drawing paper
❑ Pencil
❑ Ruler
❑ Crayons: blue, pink, orange, green, green-blue, yellow
❑ Small dish or container
❑ Black poster paint
❑ Dishwashing soap
❑ Paintbrush
❑ Tracing paper
❑ Clear tape
❑ Paper clip or metal fingernail file

1 Fold the drawing paper in half so the short ends meet to make a card. Position the card so the fold is at the top and choose 1 side as the front.

2 Use a pencil and a ruler to draw wide stripes diagonally across the card from the top left to the bottom right corner. Look at Diagram A to see what to do.

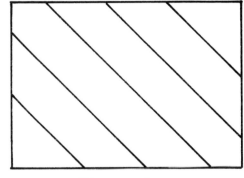

Diagram A

3 Use the crayons to color each stripe a different color. Color the stripes several times to make a thick layer of crayon.

4 Place a small amount of black poster paint in a small dish or container.

5 Add a drop of dishwashing soap to the black paint and mix well.

6 Paint the black mixture all over the thick layer of crayon on the card. (The soap helps the paint stick to the waxy crayon marks.) Let the paint dry.

7 Using tracing paper and a pencil, trace the I Love You pattern.

8 Tape the pattern to the painted card and use the pencil to trace over the pattern again. Do not tear the tracing paper. The outline of the pattern will appear on the painted card.

9 Use the open end of a paper clip or a metal fingernail file to scratch around the outline of the pattern on the card.

10 Now scratch straight lines, diagonal lines, and/or crisscross lines within the letters to make textures. Look at the photograph to see how the scratches might look.

MANY HEARTS

CHECK LIST

- ❑ 7-inch by 10-inch piece of heavy drawing paper
- ❑ Pencil
- ❑ Crayons: blue, pink, orange, green, green-blue, yellow
- ❑ Small dish or container
- ❑ Black poster paint
- ❑ Dishwashing soap
- ❑ Paintbrush
- ❑ Tracing paper
- ❑ Clear tape
- ❑ Paper clip or metal fingernail file

1 Repeat Step 1 of **I Love You**.

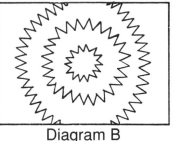
Diagram B

2 Using Diagram B as a guide, draw 4 starbursts onto the card with a pencil. Use the crayons to color each starburst a different color. Make a thick layer of crayon.

3 Repeat Steps 4, 5, and 6 of **I Love You** to paint card black.

4 Using tracing paper and a pencil, trace the 4 heart pattern. Repeat Steps 8, 9, and 10 of **I Love You**. Look at the pattern to see how to scratch the lines.

STAINED-GLASS ROSE

CHECK LIST

- ❏ 7-inch by 10-inch piece of heavy drawing paper
- ❏ 7¼-inch by 5¼-inch envelope
- ❏ Ruler
- ❏ Pencil
- ❏ Crayons: blue, pink, orange, green, green-blue, yellow
- ❏ Small dish or container
- ❏ Black poster paint
- ❏ Dishwashing soap
- ❏ Paintbrush
- ❏ Tracing paper
- ❏ Clear tape
- ❏ Paper clip or metal fingernail file

1 Fold the drawing paper in half so the short ends meet to make a card. Position the card so the fold is on the left, and choose 1 side for the front.

2 Use crayons to color the card any way you would like.

3 Use a ruler and pencil to draw a 1½-inch square in the right upper corner of the envelope front.

4 Use crayons to draw thick diagonal lines across the square in different colors.

5 Repeat Steps 4, 5, and 6 of **I Love You**, but this time, paint both the front of the card and the square on the envelope. Let the paint dry.

6 Using tracing paper and a pencil, trace the rose pattern and the heart stamp pattern.

7 Tape the rose pattern to the painted card and the heart stamp pattern to the square on the envelope.

8 Press with your pencil, tracing over the patterns again. Do not tear the tracing paper. The lines of the patterns will appear in the paint.

9 Use the open end of a paper clip or a metal fingernail file to scratch around the outlines of the patterns on the card and the envelope.

10 Scratch off nearly all of the black paint inside the rose patterns and inside the stamp heart, giving them a stained-glass look.

■ ■ ■ ■ ■ ■ ■ ■ ■ ■ ■ ■ ■

Wow your classmates when you put these cards in their Valentine boxes.

■ ■ ■ ■ ■ ■ ■ ■ ■ ■ ■ ■ ■

ROSE

HEART STAMP

Sweet Smelling Ribbons

Ribbon sachets can be used as sweet-smelling gifts that will freshen a drawer or closet. You could also display them in a decorative bowl.

Ask a grown-up to help you purchase some of the check-list items. Also ask a grown-up to help use the sewing machine.

CHECK LIST

- ❏ 4-inch by 10-inch piece of bridal netting; matching thread
- ❏ Sewing machine
- ❏ Scented bath crystals
- ❏ String
- ❏ ½ yard of 1½-inch-wide peach ribbon
- ❏ Tacky glue
- ❏ 9-inch length of ¾-inch-wide white wired ribbon
- ❏ Scissors
- ❏ ¼ yard of ¼-inch-wide peach ribbon
- ❏ Ruler

CUT & STITCH

1 Fold bridal netting in half, making the short edges meet. Fold again the other way, making the long edges meet. Now it is a 2-inch by 5-inch piece of netting.

2 Ask a grown-up to help you sew the netting into a bag. Stitch the bottom and side edges using a ¼-inch seam, but leave the top open. Turn.

3 Fill the bag with scented bath crystals and tie the top closed with string.

WRAP & GLUE

1 Wrap the wide peach ribbon vertically around the bag. Make a loop at the top on both ends of the ribbon and glue to secure. Look at the diagram.

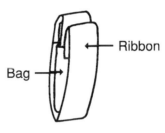

Ribbon

Bag

Diagram

2 Loop the ends of the white wired ribbon and twist in the middle to make a bow without tails.

3 Tie the narrow peach ribbon into a knot around the center of the white bow and the ribbon-covered bag near the top. Look at the photograph.

These sweet smelling ribbons are so easy to make. Make a bunch as gifts.

Kaleidoscope Scents

This potpourri bag will make any room in the house smell like a country meadow.
Experiment with different sizes and a variety of scented potpourri.
Look at the photograph on page 14.

Ask a grown-up to help you purchase some of the check-list items.

CHECK LIST

- ❏ 3-inch by 14-inch strip of white polished cotton fabric
- ❏ Scissors
- ❏ 15-inch square of white polished cotton fabric
- ❏ Spray bottle filled with water
- ❏ Acrylic paints: red, silver, blue, green, orange, yellow, purple
- ❏ 8 small containers for paint
- ❏ Wide paintbrushes
- ❏ Thin paintbrush
- ❏ 3 ounces dried potpourri

CUT & SPRAY

1 Cut each end of the fabric strip at an angle. Look at the diagram.

Diagram

2 Spray the fabric square and strip with water until damp.

3 Place a small amount of each paint, except the silver paint, in individual containers. Add water until the paints look like ink.

4 Do not add water to the silver paint and do not add water to some of the red paint. Set both aside.

PAINT & FILL

1 Paint the fabric square and strip with the watered-down colors. Let the colors run together. Cover the entire fabric with color. Let the fabric pieces dry.

2 With a wide paintbrush and undiluted paint, paint a red border along all edges on both sides of fabric square and strip.

3 With a thin paintbrush and the silver paint, paint circles, zigzags and dots. Look at the photograph. Let the paint dry.

4 Put the potpourri in the center of the fabric square. Pull up all the sides around the potpourri. Tie the fabric strip into a knot around the fabric square to make your bag.

Sneak your potpourri bag into a drawer and someone's nose will find it.

Valentine Heart Box

Everyone wants an individualized box to store special friendship notes on Valentine's Day. This box holds all your cards.
Look at the photograph on page 19.

Ask a grown-up to help you purchase some of the check-list items. Also ask a grown-up to help you use the craft knife.

CHECK LIST

- ❑ 10-inch by 11-inch heart-shaped cardboard or thin wood box with lid
- ❑ Ruler
- ❑ Pencil
- ❑ Craft knife
- ❑ Acrylic paints: red, pink
- ❑ Paintbrushes
- ❑ Paint sponges
- ❑ White paper doily
- ❑ Tracing paper
- ❑ Scrap of drawing paper
- ❑ Tacky glue

MEASURE & CUT

1 Using a ruler and pencil, measure 2 inches from the bottom point of the heart-shaped lid. Mark.

2 Turn the ruler at the diagonal toward the top right of the heart and measure 6 inches from the first mark. Mark.

3 Draw a line from the first to the second mark. Then, draw another line parallel to that line about ¼ inch above it. Connect the lines at each end so a rectangle is marked on the lid.

4 Ask a grown-up to help you cut out the rectangle with a craft knife. This makes a slot to drop cards into the box.

PAINT & TRACE

1 Using a paintbrush, paint the box and the lid red. Let the paint dry.

2 Using the pink paint, paint a ½-inch border around the top of the lid and paint connecting V-shapes along the edges of the lid for trim. Look at the photograph to see how this should look.

3 Now use pink paint to paint your name (or the name of a friend) above the slot in the box lid. Again, look at the photograph.

4 With a sponge, paint the doily and 1 side of the drawing paper pink. Let the paint dry.

5 Using tracing paper and a pencil, trace the heart pattern. Cut out the pattern.

6 Place the heart pattern on the pink drawing paper. Trace and cut out 3 hearts.

CUT & GLUE

1 Place the pink doily over the left top of the heart-shaped lid. With a pencil, trace the top left curve of the lid onto the doily.

2 Cut along the pencil line and discard the outside, cut-away edge of the doily. Look at the photograph.

3 Glue the remaining part of the doily onto the top left part of the lid.

4 Glue the 3 hearts under the slot cut into the right half of the lid.

As a special Valentine's gift, you could make some heart boxes for your friends.

HEART

18

Rose Petal Sachet

*Fresh rose petals will dry but continue to provide the scent
for a unique sachet ball made out of crochet thread.
People will wonder how you got the petals in there!*

**Ask a grown-up to help you purchase
some of the check-list items.**

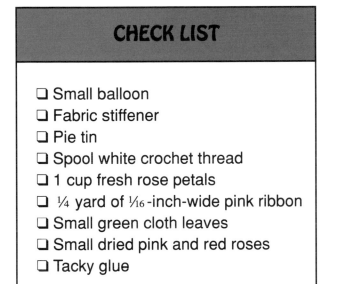

CHECK LIST

- ❑ Small balloon
- ❑ Fabric stiffener
- ❑ Pie tin
- ❑ Spool white crochet thread
- ❑ 1 cup fresh rose petals
- ❑ ¼ yard of ¹⁄₁₆-inch-wide pink ribbon
- ❑ Small green cloth leaves
- ❑ Small dried pink and red roses
- ❑ Tacky glue

INFLATE & WRAP

1 Inflate the balloon so it is about 3 inches wide.

2 Pour the fabric stiffener into the pie tin, and pull the crochet thread through the fabric stiffener.

3 Wrap the thread around the balloon, overlapping the thread so the balloon is completely covered, except for a small circle, about ½ inch wide, at the top.

4 When the thread is completely dry, pop the balloon and pull it out between the thread. Pull slowly and carefully so you do not damage the thread ball.

FILL & GLUE

1 Fill the ball with fresh rose petals. These will dry in the thread ball but will continue to be sweet-smelling.

2 Thread 1 end of the pink ribbon through some of the threads near the small hole on top of the ball. Loop the ribbon and tie it to make a hanger.

3 Glue the cloth leaves and dried roses around the top of the ball, covering the hole. Look at the photograph to see how this should look.

The sachet ball can hang in the closet, the bathroom or in a window.

Thumb-Body Plate

*If you want to put your unique signature or mark on something,
stamp it with your thumb print. No one else in the world
has the same thumb print as you!*

Ask a grown-up to help you purchase some of the check-list items.

CHECK LIST

❏ 8-inch-round wood plate
❏ 10-inch-round wood plate
❏ 5 small star wood cutouts
❏ 1-inch heart wood cutout
❏ Acrylic paints: white, red, light blue
❏ Paint sponges
❏ Narrow paintbrush
❏ Wood glue

PAINT

1 With a sponge, paint both of the plates white.

2 Paint the star cutouts white and the heart cutout red. Let the paint dry.

3 With a sponge, paint light blue over the outer border area of the large plate.

4 Sponge the light blue paint lightly over the white paint on the plates, letting some of the white paint show through.

5 With the paintbrush, paint 2 thin red lines around the borders of each plate.

PRINT & GLUE

1 Using a narrow paintbrush and red paint, print the words "Thumb-body Loves You" in the middle of the smaller plate. If you want, make a heart for the "o" in the word "loves." Look at the photograph to see how to space the letters.

2 Put some light blue paint on your thumb and then, press your thumb lightly onto the small plate under the words. Let the paint dry.

3 Glue the heart and stars around the outer border of the large plate, as shown in the photograph.

4 Place the small plate in the center of the large plate and glue them together.

**You've made a 1-of-a-kind plate
to show off in the kitchen.**

23

Bean-Bag Bunny

You can toss this bunny for lots of good times.
The candy carrot might belong to the bunny but you could
have some of the candy since you made them both.

Ask a grown-up to help you purchase some of the check-list items. Also ask a grown-up to help you use the sewing machine.

CHECK LIST

- ❑ 12-inch square of yellow plastic cellophane
- ❑ Clear tape
- ❑ ½ cup hard fruit-shaped candies
- ❑ ½ yard of ½-inch-wide green gift ribbon
- ❑ Scissors
- ❑ Tracing paper
- ❑ Pencil
- ❑ Straight pins
- ❑ 20-inch square blue polished cotton fabric
- ❑ 10-inch square of white felt; matching thread
- ❑ Pinking shears
- ❑ Sewing machine
- ❑ Needle and thread
- ❑ 2 cups small dry beans
- ❑ Polyester stuffing
- ❑ ½ yard of 2-inch-wide white lace
- ❑ Assorted miniature plastic cutouts
- ❑ 2 small plastic star cutouts
- ❑ Tacky glue

ROLL & FILL

1 Roll the yellow cellophane square from 1 corner toward the other corner to make a 2½-inch-wide, cone-shaped carrot. Use clear tape to attach the edges and the bottom.

2 Fill the cone with candy.

3 Tie the green gift ribbon around the top. Cut and curl the ribbon any way you would like.

TRACE & CUT

1 Using tracing paper and a pencil, trace the body, head, face, hand, and foot patterns on pages 26 and 27.

2 Pin the body pattern to the blue fabric and cut out 2 body pieces.

3 Pin the head, face, hand, and foot patterns to the white felt. Using pinking shears, cut out 1 head, 2 faces, 2 hands, and 2 feet.

STUFF & SEW

1 Ask a grown-up to help you sew the body pieces together. With the right sides of the blue fabric facing, place the hands and the feet between the 2 body pieces in the places indicated on the pattern. With a ¼-inch seam, stitch the sides and bottom, securing the hands and feet in the seams.

2 Fold the top raw edges to the inside and hem. Sew gathering threads along the top edge. Gathering threads are 2 rows of long, loose stitches spaced about ¼ inch apart and parallel to each other.

3 Turn the body inside out, and then fill the body with beans. Set the bean body aside for a while.

4 For the face, place the 2 face pieces together with right sides facing and stitch a center front seam. Turn inside out.

5 Match the face piece to the head piece. With the wrong sides facing, topstitch these pieces together, leaving the bottom edges open.

6 Fill the head with polyester stuffing.

7 Stitch the bottom edges of the head together.

STITCH & GLUE

1 Gather the top edge of the body fabric to fit into the bottom edge of the head. Insert the head into the top of the body and handstitch together.

2 Sew gathering threads along the lengthwise center of the lace piece. Gather to fit around the area where the head meets the body.

3 Wrap the gathered lace around the neck area and stitch the short ends together to make a secure collar.

4 Glue the 2 stars to the face for eyes.

5 Glue the other plastic cutouts to the blue body fabric. Look at the photograph to see how this might look.

A bean-bag bunny will last through many tossing games but the sweets go quickly.

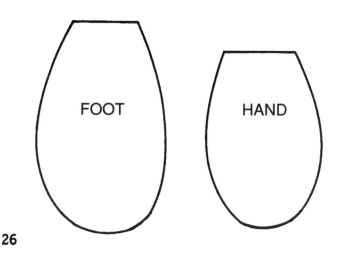

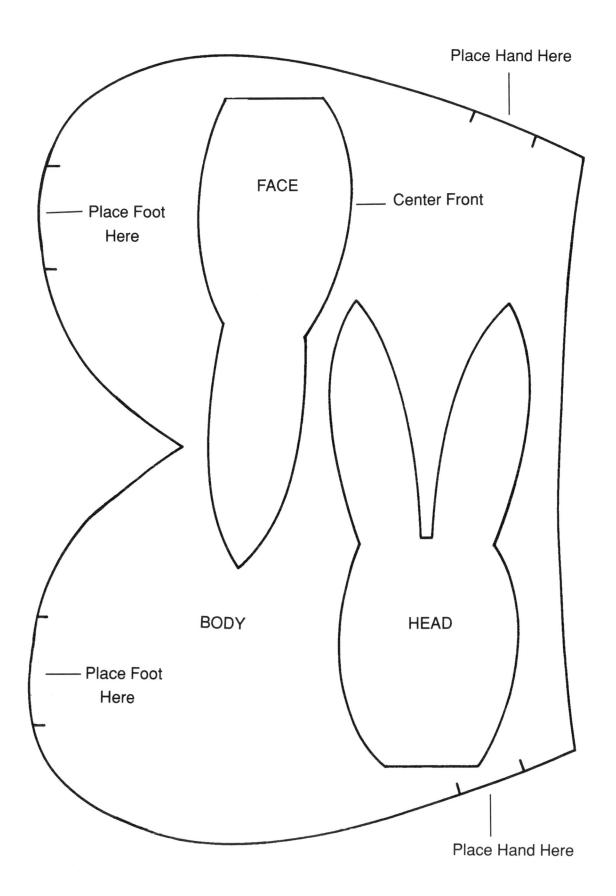

Place Hand Here

Place Foot
Here

FACE

Center Front

BODY

HEAD

Place Foot
Here

Place Hand Here

27

Fun Full of Holes

Making a shelf liner, ornaments or a wreath is easy when you use paint and some well-placed holes. This technique gives your crafts an extra punch!

Ask a grown-up to help you purchase some of the check-list items.

NIFTY SHELF LINER

CHECK LIST

- ❏ Tracing paper
- ❏ Pencil
- ❏ Scissors
- ❏ Watercolor paper
- ❏ Watercolor paints: red, blue, green, yellow, purple, pink, orange
- ❏ Paintbrushes
- ❏ Color pencils: red, blue, green, yellow, purple, pink, orange
- ❏ Small-hole paper punch
- ❏ Tacky glue
- ❏ 18-inch by ⅝-inch wood molding strip
- ❏ Green acrylic paint

1 Using tracing paper and a pencil, trace the rabbit and carrot patterns on page 30. Cut them out.

2 Place the patterns on the watercolor paper, trace around them, and cut out 4 rabbits and 12 carrots.

3 Paint both sides of the cutouts any color you would like. Let the paint dry.

4 Use a pencil of the same color to outline the edges of the rabbits and carrots as shown on the patterns.

5 Using a paper punch, make holes where indicated on the patterns.

6 Paint the flat wood molding strip green. Let the paint dry.

7 Glue the rabbits and carrots to the wood. Look at the photograph to see how to place them.

8 Glue the liner to the front of a shelf.

CARROT PATCH WREATH

CHECK LIST

❑ Tracing paper
❑ Pencil
❑ Scissors
❑ Watercolor paper
❑ Watercolor paints: red, blue, green, yellow, purple, pink, orange
❑ Paintbrushes
❑ Color pencils: red, blue, green, yellow, purple, pink, orange
❑ Small-hole paper punch
❑ 6¼-inch wood circle wreath
❑ White acrylic paint
❑ Tacky glue
❑ Ruler
❑ 2-inch-long, ¼-inch-wide, ⅛-inch-thick foam strip

1 Repeat Steps 1, 2, 3, 4, and 5 of **Nifty Shelf Liner,** cutting out 24 carrots and 2 rabbits.

2 Paint the wood circle white. Let the paint dry.

3 Glue 20 carrots around the circle frame any way you would like. Look at the the photograph on page 28.

4 Cut the foam strip into 6 pieces, each measuring ¼ inch square.

5 Glue 1 foam square to the back of each of the 2 rabbits and the back of the 4 remaining carrots.

6 Place glue on the foam square attached to the rabbits and carrots.

7 Attach the rabbits to the center bottom of the wreath and the carrots anywhere you would like. Look at the photograph.

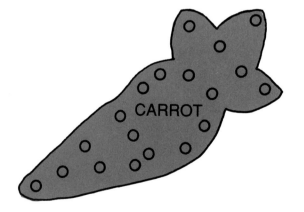

CARROT

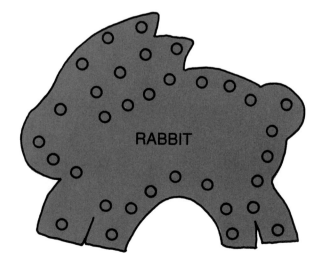

RABBIT

PUNCHY ORNAMENTS

CHECK LIST

❑ Tracing paper
❑ Pencil
❑ Scissors
❑ Watercolor paper
❑ Watercolor paints: red, blue, green, yellow, purple, pink, orange
❑ Paintbrushes
❑ Color pencils: red, blue, green, yellow, purple, pink, orange
❑ Small-hole paper punch
❑ Tacky glue
❑ Ruler
❑ 2 yards of ¹⁄₁₆-inch-wide satin ribbon in different colors: red, blue, green, yellow, purple, pink, orange

1 Using tracing paper and a pencil, trace the rabbit and carrot patterns on page 30. Cut them out.

2 Place the patterns on the watercolor paper and trace around them. Trace and cut out a total of 8 pieces.

3 Repeat Steps 3, 4, and 5 from **Nifty Shelf Liner**.

4 Cut satin ribbon into 8 pieces, each 9 inches long.

5 Pull 1 end of 1 ribbon piece through a hole in a rabbit or carrot ornament. Bring the ends together and tie in a knot near the ends of the ribbon. Repeat to make hangers for all of the paper ornaments. Look at the photograph on page 31.

You now have 3 different types of crafts full of extra punch. Try to think of others.

32

Rings From The Sky

Make color-coordinated napkin rings with sky patterns to add a star quality to the dinner table. Look at the photograph on page 34.

Ask a grown-up to help you purchase some of the check-list items. Also ask a grown-up to help you use the craft knife and hot glue gun.

CHECK LIST

- ❏ Tracing paper
- ❏ Pencil
- ❏ Carbon paper
- ❏ Clear tape
- ❏ 3-inch by 36-inch piece of balsa wood
- ❏ Craft knife
- ❏ 4 wood napkin rings
- ❏ 14-inch-square cloth napkins: burgundy, orange, blue, green
- ❏ Acrylic paints: burgundy, orange, blue, green
- ❏ Wide paintbrushes
- ❏ Fine-grade sandpaper
- ❏ Hot glue gun and glue sticks

TRACE & CUT

1 Using tracing paper and a pencil, trace the sun, moon, and star patterns on page 35.

2 Tape the carbon paper to the balsa wood with the carbon side down. Tape the traced patterns over the carbon paper.

3 Trace around the patterns again. The carbon paper will transfer the shapes to the balsa wood. Trace 1 sunburst, 1 circle, 1 moon, and 2 stars on the wood.

4 Ask a grown-up to help cut out the shapes using the craft knife. Cut gently because balsa wood is fragile and can break if you press too hard.

PAINT & SAND

1 Paint 1 napkin ring, the sun, and the circle burgundy. Let the paint dry.

2 Paint 1 napkin ring and the moon orange. Let the paint dry.

3 Paint 1 star and 1 napkin ring with blue paint and the other star and napkin ring with green paint. Let the paint dry.

4 Using the sandpaper, sand each shape and napkin ring along the edges. Look at the photograph to see how this should look. Sanding off some of the paint gives the shapes a worn look.

GLUE & ASSEMBLE

1 Ask a grown-up to help with the hot glue gun. Glue the circle to the middle of the sun shape. Glue the sun shape to its matching napkin ring.

2 Glue the moon shape to its matching napkin ring.

3 Glue each star shape to its matching napkin ring.

4 Fold the napkins and pull each through the napkin ring of the same color.

**You now have 4 napkin rings
taken from the sky.
What a heavenly dining design!**

CIRCLE

SUNBURST

MOON

STAR

35

Heaven's Greeting

The sun and the moon rise and set, never meeting each other.
You can bring them together in this artistic floor cloth.

Ask a grown-up to help you purchase some of the check-list items.

CHECK LIST

- ❑ 40-inch square of heavy canvas
- ❑ Pencil
- ❑ Yardstick
- ❑ Acrylic paints: white, blue, gold, navy, red, black, pink
- ❑ Narrow and wide sponge brushes
- ❑ Narrow and wide paintbrushes
- ❑ Tracing paper
- ❑ Scissors
- ❑ Fabric chalk
- ❑ 6 clothespins
- ❑ Tacky glue
- ❑ Clear latex wood finish

MEASURE & MARK

1 Fold the canvas square in half 1 way and then the other way so it is divided into 4 parts. Unfold. With a pencil, mark the center where folds come to a point.

2 Using a yardstick, measure 6 inches out from the center dot and mark. Measure in several places, making marks to form a circle.

3 Connect the marks to make a 12-inch-wide circle in the center of the canvas. (You could make this circle by using a compass, or even by tracing around a large dinner plate, but you will have to follow the measuring-and-marking system for larger circles.)

4 Next measure 14 inches out from the center dot in several places and mark each place. Connect the marks to make a 28-inch-wide circle.

5 Now measure 15 inches out from the center dot to several places and mark each place. Connect the dots to make a 30-inch-wide circle.

6 Use the yardstick to draw a straight line through the center of the circles from the top to the bottom.

TRACE & PAINT

1 Using a sponge brush, paint the left half of the small circle white. Before the paint dries, sponge paint blue over the white, smearing the colors together.

2 Using a sponge brush, paint the right half of the small center circle gold. Let the paint dry.

3 Paint the left half of the outside circle navy and the right half of the circle white. Let the paint dry.

4 Using tracing paper and a pencil, trace the star pattern and cut it out.

5 Place the star pattern on the navy half-circle and, using the fabric chalk, trace around the pattern. Do this about 16 to 18 times on different parts of the navy half-circle. Look at the photograph to see how to arrange the stars.

6 Using a paintbrush, paint all the stars gold. Let the paint dry. Apply a second coat, if needed, to make the stars bright.

7 Using wide paintbrushes, paint wavy lines coming out from around the small gold half circle. Alternate using gold and red paint. Make about 20 lines all together. Again, look at the photograph to see how this should look.

8 Outline the small circle with black paint. Then, using the photograph as a guide, draw the face with fabric chalk.

9 With your finger, smear red paint in a circle to make the cheeks. Paint the mouth pink. Paint the eyes black. Let the paint dry.

STAR

CUT & GLUE

1 Cut the large circle from the canvas.

2 Cut slits, about ½ inch long, around the edge of the circle. Make the slits about 1 inch apart.

3 Fold about 1 inch around the edge of the canvas down to the plain side and glue the pieces. Overlap as needed to make a smooth circular edge for the front.

4 Use clothespins to hold the hem to the back until the glue is dry. Work on small sections at a time until the entire circle hem is complete and the glue is dry.

5 Use a sponge brush to apply the latex wood finish to cover the front of the floor cloth. Let the finish dry.

**The day/night face is finished.
Treat it well and the cloth will last
for a long time.**

Pots With Pizzazz

Not your grandma's plain, reddish-brown planting pots—these clay pots are all dressed up to coordinate with bright colors in your room or house.

Ask a grown-up to help you purchase some of the check-list items.

WHITE POT

CHECK LIST

- ❑ 6-inch by 5¼-inch clay pot with base
- ❑ White acrylic paint
- ❑ Paint sponge
- ❑ Clear spray resin
- ❑ Plastic stencil with numerous shapes
- ❑ 2-inch-wide vinyl tape: blue, red, green, yellow, orange, purple
- ❑ Tracing paper
- ❑ Pencil
- ❑ Scissors

1 Using a sponge and white paint, paint the clay pot and base. Let the paint dry.

2 Spray the pot and base with clear resin. Let the resin dry.

3 Using the stencil of shapes, trace 10 or more shapes onto each color of vinyl tape. Cut out the shapes.

4 Stick the shapes onto the white pot any way you would like, overlapping some of them. Look at the photograph to see how this should look.

5 Spray another coat of clear resin over the pot and base. Let the resin dry.

RED POT

CHECK LIST

- ❑ 6-inch by 5¼-inch clay pot with base
- ❑ Red acrylic paint
- ❑ Paint sponge
- ❑ Plastic stencil with numerous shapes
- ❑ Tracing paper
- ❑ Pencil
- ❑ Clear tape
- ❑ Clear spray resin
- ❑ 8 purchased cow stickers
- ❑ Scissors
- ❑ Tacky glue

1 Using a sponge and red paint, paint the clay pot and base. Let the paint dry.

2 Spray the pot and base with clear resin. Let the resin dry.

3 Using tracing paper and a pencil, trace the heart pattern.

4 Tape the heart pattern to 4 of the cow stickers and cut out 1 heart from each cow shape.

5 Glue the 4 cow stickers and 4 hearts to the red pot. Look at the photograph to see how you should place the cutouts.

6 Spray another coat of resin over the pot and base. Let the resin dry.

BLUE POT

CHECK LIST

- ❑ 6-inch by 5¼-inch clay pot with base
- ❑ Blue acrylic paint
- ❑ Paint sponge
- ❑ Clear spray resin
- ❑ 35 yards of ⅛-inch-wide blue satin cording
- ❑ Scissors
- ❑ Tacky glue

1 Using a sponge and blue paint, paint the clay pot and base. Let the paint dry.

2 Spray the pot and base with clear resin. Let the resin dry.

3 Glue 1 end of the blue satin cording to the top lip of the pot.

4 Wrap the cording around the pot from top to bottom, gluing as you go. Make sure that you wrap the cording close together.

5 Wrap and glue the blue cording around the base.

HEART
Cut 4

YELLOW POT

CHECK LIST

- ❏ 6-inch by 5¼-inch clay pot with base
- ❏ Yellow acrylic paint
- ❏ Paint sponge
- ❏ Clear spray resin
- ❏ ¾-inch-wide green vinyl tape
- ❏ Scissors

1 Using a sponge and yellow paint, paint the pot and base. Let the paint dry.

2 Spray the pot and base with clear resin. Let the resin dry

3 Beginning at the top edge of the pot, wrap the green tape in a spiral around the pot, leaving a wide space between the rows of tape as you go. Look at the photograph to see the striped pattern.

4 Wrap the tape around the base.

5 Spray another coat of resin over the pot and the base. Let the resin dry.

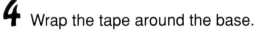

Fill your pots with live houseplants or use them to hold favorite treasures.

NOTE: We give a list of items needed and instructions for 4 different pots, but you can mix-and-match pots and designs to make your own special pot.

Egg Popper Surprise

These cute egghead cones are filled with surprises for you and your friends.

Ask a grown-up to help you purchase some of the check-list items.

GENTLEMAN CAT

CHECK LIST

- ❑ Large egg
- ❑ Small, sharp nail
- ❑ Straight pin
- ❑ Multi-colored confetti
- ❑ Assorted small wrapped candies
- ❑ Balloon
- ❑ Clear tape
- ❑ Pencil
- ❑ Tracing paper
- ❑ Carbon paper
- ❑ Black fine-tip permanent marker
- ❑ Scrap black felt
- ❑ Pink acrylic paint
- ❑ Paintbrush
- ❑ 2 blue confetti stars
- ❑ Access to a copy machine
- ❑ Tacky glue
- ❑ Sheet drawing paper
- ❑ Blue watercolor paint
- ❑ 1½-inch-wide yellow vinyl tape
- ❑ ¼-inch-wide yellow vinyl tape
- ❑ ¼ yard of ¼-inch-wide yellow ribbon

MAKE EGGHEAD

1 Use the nail to poke a small hole in the center of the narrow end of an egg. Enlarge the hole to about ½ inch round. Then, use a pin to poke a tiny hole in the other end of the egg.

2 Drain the contents of the egg and flush the inside of the shell with water. Let the egg dry.

3 Fill the egg shell with confetti, a small piece of wrapped candy, and a balloon. Use clear tape to close the opening.

4 Using tracing paper and a pencil, trace the cat face pattern on page 46.

5 Tape the carbon paper to the egg with the carbon side touching the egg's surface. Tape the traced cat face pattern over the carbon paper and retrace the face. The carbon paper will transfer the pattern to the egg

6 Outline the face with a black marker.

7 Trace the cat ear pattern on page 46. Pin the pattern to the felt and cut out 2 ears.

8 Paint a pink triangle in the middle of each felt ear.

9 Glue the ears to the top of the egg, and glue the confetti stars on for eyes.

MAKE CONE

1 Using tracing paper and a pencil, trace the cone pattern on page 51.

2 Fold the cone pattern in half vertically. Set the photocopying machine at 140%. Copy the first half of the pattern. Repeat with the second half. Tape the two halves together. Cut out the cone pattern.

3 Place this pattern on the drawing paper and trace around it. Cut it out.

4 Paint the paper cone with the blue watercolor paint. Let the paint dry.

5 Trace the star pattern and cut it out.

6 Place the pattern on the wide yellow vinyl tape and cut out 8 stars.

7 Stick the stars onto the blue paper.

8 Roll the blue paper into a cone so the widest end has an opening about 1½ inches. Glue the cone to secure.

9 Fill the cone with wrapped candies.

ASSEMBLE PARTS

1 Insert a small part of the narrow taped end of the egg in the cone. Be sure that most of the egg shows above the cone.

2 Use the narrow yellow vinyl tape to tape the egg and cone together.

3 Tie the yellow ribbon into a bow and glue it to the front so it is centered on the vinyl tape. Look at the photograph to see how this might look.

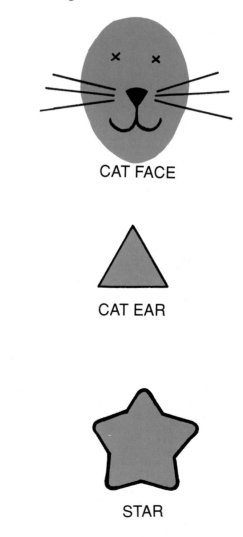

CAT FACE

CAT EAR

STAR

WIGGLE PIG

CHECK LIST

- ❏ Large egg
- ❏ Small, sharp nail
- ❏ Straight pin
- ❏ Multi-colored confetti
- ❏ Assorted small individually wrapped candies
- ❏ Balloon
- ❏ Clear tape
- ❏ Pencil
- ❏ Tracing paper
- ❏ Carbon paper
- ❏ Black fine-tip permanent marker
- ❏ Scrap pink felt
- ❏ 2 purple confetti hearts
- ❏ Tacky glue
- ❏ Sheet drawing paper
- ❏ Purple watercolor paint
- ❏ Paintbrush
- ❏ 1½-inch-wide purple vinyl tape
- ❏ ¼-inch-wide purple vinyl tape
- ❏ Scrap purple tissue paper

MAKE EGGHEAD

1 Repeat "Make Egghead" Steps 1, 2, and 3 of the **Gentleman Cat** to drain and fill the egg.

2 Using tracing paper and a pencil, trace the pig face pattern and then transfer it to the egg and outline it, following Steps 5 and 6 of **Gentleman Cat.**

3 Trace the pig ear pattern. Pin the pattern to the pink felt and cut out 2 ears.

4 Glue the tips of the ears down. Look at the photograph to see how this should look. Glue the ears to top back of the egg, and glue confetti hearts on for the eyes.

PIG FACE

PIG EAR

HEART

MAKE CONE

1 Repeat "Make Cone" Steps 1 and 2 of **Gentleman Cat** to trace, copy, and cut out the cone.

2 Paint the cone with purple watercolor paint. Let the paint dry.

3 Using tracing paper and a pencil, trace the heart pattern on page 47. Cut it out.

4 Position the heart pattern on the wide purple vinyl tape. Trace and cut 8 hearts.

5 Stick the hearts onto the purple paper.

6 Roll the paper to form a cone and fill the cone by repeating Steps 8 and 9 of **Gentleman Cat**.

ASSEMBLE PARTS

1 Insert a small portion of the taped end of the egg in the cone.

2 Insert a gathered piece of purple tissue paper between the egg and the cone so the edges form a collar. Glue.

3 Use the narrow purple vinyl tape to tape the egg and cone together.

MUCH-ADO MOUSE

CHECK LIST

- ❑ Large egg
- ❑ Small, sharp nail
- ❑ Straight pin
- ❑ Multi-colored confetti
- ❑ Assorted small individually wrapped candies
- ❑ Balloon
- ❑ Clear tape
- ❑ Pencil
- ❑ Tracing paper
- ❑ Carbon paper
- ❑ Black fine-tip permanent marker
- ❑ Scrap grey felt
- ❑ Pink acrylic paint
- ❑ Paintbrush
- ❑ 2 purple confetti stars
- ❑ Tacky glue
- ❑ Sheet drawing paper
- ❑ 12-inch square of wrapping paper
- ❑ ¼-inch-wide green vinyl tape
- ❑ Scrap pink tissue paper

1 Repeat "Make Egghead" Steps 1, 2, and 3 of the **Gentleman Cat** to drain and fill the egg.

2 Trace the rabbit/mouse face pattern and cut it out. Transfer the pattern to the egg and outline the face by repeating Steps 4 and 5 of **Gentleman Cat**.

3 Trace the mouse ear pattern and cut it out. Pin the pattern to the grey felt and cut out 2 ears.

4 Paint the center of each ear pink. Let the paint dry.

5 Glue the ears to the top of the egg, and glue the confetti stars on for the eyes.

6 Repeat "Make Cone" Steps 1 and 2 of **Gentleman Cat** to trace, copy, and cut out the cone.

7 Position the cone pattern on the drawing paper and cut out 1 cone. Then, position the pattern on the wrapping paper and cut out another cone.

8 Glue the wrapping paper and drawing paper cone patterns together.

9 Form the cone and fill it by repeating Steps 8 and 9 of **Gentleman Cat**.

10 Insert a small portion of the egg into the cone.

11 Insert a gathered piece of pink tissue paper between the egg and cone so the edges form a collar. Glue.

12 Use the green vinyl tape to tape the egg and cone together.

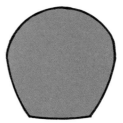

RABBIT/MOUSE FACE

MOUSE EAR

WACKY WABBIT

CHECK LIST

- ❏ Large egg
- ❏ Small, sharp nail
- ❏ Straight pin
- ❏ Multi-colored confetti
- ❏ Assorted small individually wrapped candies
- ❏ Balloon
- ❏ Clear tape
- ❏ Pencil
- ❏ Tracing paper
- ❏ Carbon paper
- ❏ Black fine-tip permanent marker
- ❏ Scrap white felt
- ❏ Pink acrylic paint
- ❏ Paintbrush
- ❏ 2 red confetti hearts
- ❏ Tacky glue
- ❏ Sheet drawing paper
- ❏ Red acrylic paint
- ❏ Paint sponge
- ❏ ¼-inch-wide red vinyl tape

RABBIT EAR

1 Repeat "Make Egghead" Steps 1, 2, and 3 of the **Gentleman Cat**.

2 Trace the rabbit/mouse face pattern on page 49 and cut it out. Repeat Steps 5 and 6 of **Gentleman Cat**.

3 Trace the rabbit ear pattern and cut it out. Pin the pattern to the white felt and cut out 2 ears.

4 Paint the center of the ears pink. Let the paint dry.

5 Glue the ears to the top back of the egg, and glue confetti hearts on for eyes.

6 Repeat "Make Cone" Steps 1, 2, and 3 of **Gentleman Cat**.

7 Use a sponge to paint the cone with the red acrylic paint. Let the paint dry. Make the cone shape and fill the cone with candy following "Make Cone" Steps 8 and 9 of **Gentleman Cat**.

8 Insert a small portion of the taped end of the egg into the cone.

9 Use the red vinyl tape to tape the egg and cone together.

These egghead cones make great fun, so give them to your friends as special goodies at a party.

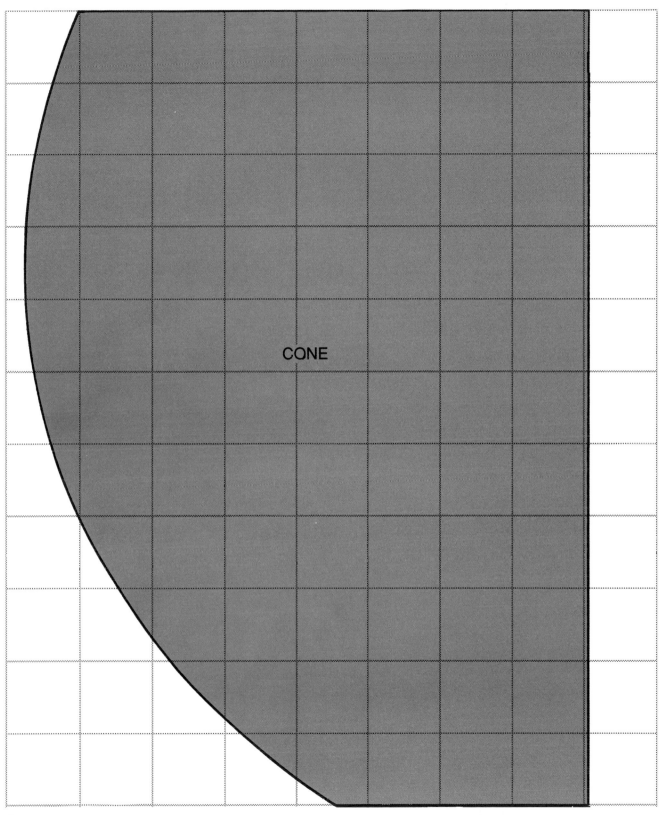

CONE

1 square = 1 inch

Uncommon Bird Houses

*These decorative bird nests are unique: a cat's mouth
that's not too safe and a sweet watermelon shack.*

**Ask a grown-up to help you purchase
some of the check-list items.**

KITTY GOTCHA?

CHECK LIST

❏ Access to a copy machine that
  enlarges
❏ Tracing paper
❏ Pencil
❏ 15-inch square of 2-inch-thick craft
  foam
❏ Table knife
❏ 6-inch craft foam ball
❏ Spanish moss
❏ Small craft bird
❏ 2-inch-long twig
❏ Tacky glue
❏ Paintbrushes
❏ Acrylic paints: white, gray, black,
  pink, green

---

1 Using tracing paper and a pencil,
trace the cat pattern on page 56.

2 Fold the cat pattern in half vertically.
Set the copy machine at 200%. Copy the
first half of the pattern. Copy the second
half. Tape the two halves together. Cut
out the pattern.

3 Position this pattern on the craft foam
square and trace around it.

4 Use a table knife carefully and cut out
the cat pattern. Also cut out the circle as
shown on the pattern.

5 Take the foam ball and hollow out a
hole the same size as the circle.

6 Glue the ball to the back of the cat,
so the opening in the ball matches the
circle in the cat cutout.

7 Paint the cat white and gray as
indicated on the pattern. Paint the nose
and inside of the ears pink. Paint the eyes
black and green. Look at the photograph.
Let the paint dry.

8 Put a drop of glue on 1 end of the twig
and push the twig about 1 inch into the
foam cat just below the hole.

9 Glue the moss into the hole. Glue the
bird to the twig. Look at the photograph to
see how this should look.

BIRDIE SEED SNACK

CHECK LIST

- ❏ Access to a copy machine that enlarges
- ❏ Tracing paper
- ❏ Pencil
- ❏ 15-inch square of 2-inch-thick craft foam
- ❏ Table knife
- ❏ 6-inch craft foam ball
- ❏ Spanish moss
- ❏ Small craft bird
- ❏ 2-inch-long twig
- ❏ Tacky glue
- ❏ Paintbrushes
- ❏ Acrylic paints: green, red, black

1 Using tracing paper and a pencil, trace the watermelon pattern on page 57.

2 Fold the watermelon pattern in half vertically. Set the copy machine at 140%. Copy the first half of the pattern. Copy the second half. Tape the two halves together. Cut out the pattern.

3 Position this pattern on the craft foam square and trace around it.

4 Use a table knife carefully to cut out the watermelon pattern. Also cut out the circle from the watermelon where the pattern indicates.

5 Take the foam ball and hollow out a hole the same size as the circle shown on the watermelon pattern.

6 Glue the ball to the back of the watermelon, matching the hollow in the ball to the circle on the watermelon.

7 Paint the watermelon green and red with black seeds. Look at the photograph. Let the paint dry.

8 Paint the inside of the watermelon nest red. Let the paint dry.

9 Put a drop of glue on 1 end of the twig. Push the twig about 1 inch into the watermelon below the nest hole.

10 Glue the moss into the hole. Glue the bird to the twig.

Hanging outside or indoors, these nests will bring a smile to every face.

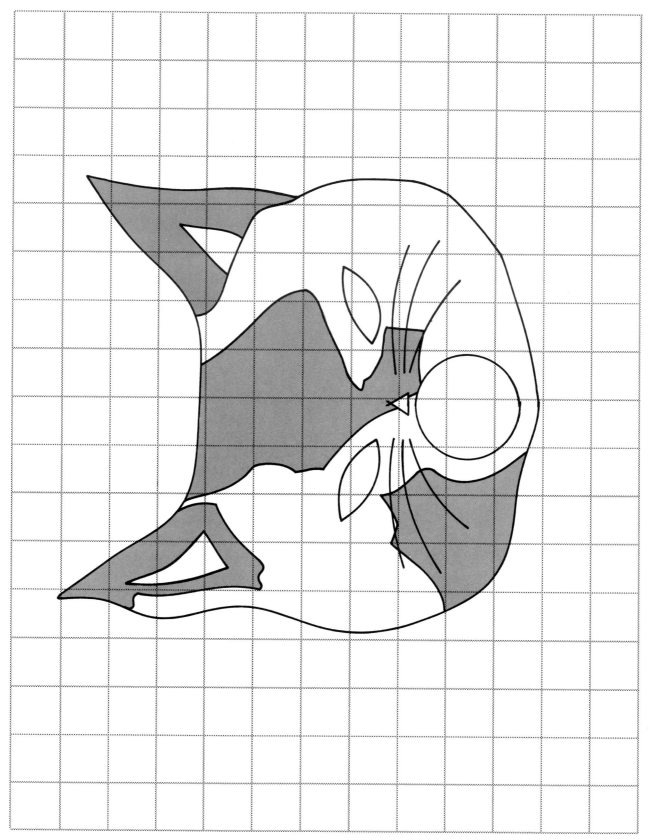

1 square = 1 inch

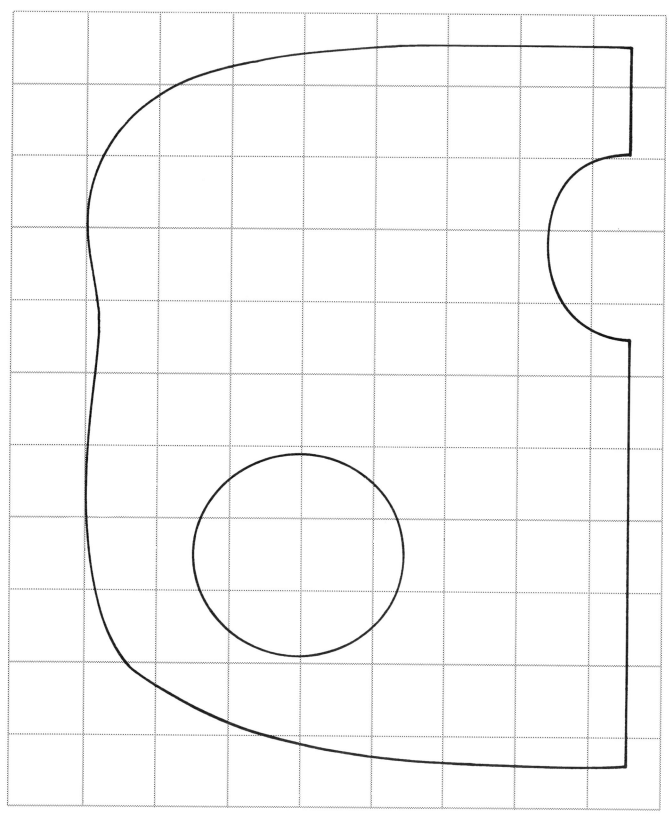

1 square = 1 inch

Decorated Gloves

Give these colorful gloves to any of your car-owning friends or family members. Or wear them yourself when helping to pump gas.

Ask a grown-up to help you purchase some of the check-list items. Also ask a grown-up to help you use the sewing machine.

RED WHEELS

CHECK LIST

- ❏ Pair of bright floral-patterned garden gloves
- ❏ Measuring tape
- ❏ Scissors
- ❏ Needle and thread
- ❏ Sewing machine
- ❏ 1 yard of 3-inch-wide ivory eyelet
- ❏ 2 plastic yellow star buttons
- ❏ 2 red plaid cloth appliqué bows
- ❏ 2 small cloth appliqué roses
- ❏ 8 small red wheel buttons

1 Use the tape measure to measure around the cuff of 1 glove. Double the measurement.

2 Cut the eyelet into 2 pieces, each piece the length you calculated in Step 1.

3 With a needle and thread, stitch gathering threads along the straight edge of each ivory eyelet piece and gather to fit the cuff of each glove.

4 Ask a grown-up to help you use the sewing machine. Stitch the short ends of each piece of eyelet together.

5 With the right sides facing, stitch the eyelet pieces to the cuff on each glove.

6 With a needle and thread, stitch a red plaid appliqué bow to the center top front of each glove.

7 Stitch a yellow star button in the middle of each bow.

8 Stitch a rose appliqué to each glove near the plaid bow.

9 Stitch 4 red wheels along the eyelet seam centered horizontally on the front of each glove.

■●★ ■●★ ■●★ ■●★ ■

What a nice gift! Or keep them for yourself and have some colorful fun at play time.

■●★ ■●★ ■●★ ■●★ ■

Dream Messages

You'll actually want to go to bed at night when you have a big, bright pillow case to cushion your sleepy head. You can even personalize one with a name.

Ask a grown-up to help you purchase some of the check-list items. Also ask a grown-up to help you use the iron.

RED WISH

CHECK LIST
❑ ½ yard blue/white checked fabric
❑ 1 yard iron-on, paper-backed transfer web
❑ Iron
❑ Tracing paper
❑ Pencil
❑ Access to a copy machine that enlarges
❑ Scissors
❑ Red pillow case

1 Ask a grown-up to help you iron the transfer web to the blue/white checked fabric. Iron the paper surface so the web becomes fused to the fabric.

2 Using tracing paper and a pencil, trace the letters for "Good Night" from the alphabet on pages 188.

3 Using a copy machine, enlarge the letters so each is 4 inches high.

4 Cut out the letters from the paper.

5 Place the letters backwards on the paper side of the transfer web, trace around them, and cut out the letters. Then, remove the paper.

6 Position the letters on the pillow case with the transfer web down on the fabric. Look at the photograph to see how to arrange the letters.

7 Ask a grown-up to help you iron the letters onto the pillow case.

FRENCH BLUE

CHECK LIST

- ❑ ½ yard white-dotted red fabric
- ❑ 1 yard iron-on, paper-backed transfer web
- ❑ Iron
- ❑ Tracing paper
- ❑ Pencil
- ❑ Access to a copy machine that enlarges
- ❑ Scissors
- ❑ Blue pillow case

1 Ask a grown-up to help you iron the transfer web to the white-dotted red fabric. Iron the paper surface so the web becomes fused to the fabric.

2 Using tracing paper and a pencil, trace the letters for "La Nuit," which means "Good Night" in French, from the alphabet on page 188.

3 Repeat Steps 3, 4, 5, 6, and 7 from **Red Wish**.

NAVY NAME

CHECK LIST

- ❑ ½ yard white fabric
- ❑ 1 yard iron-on, paper-backed transfer web
- ❑ Iron
- ❑ Tracing paper
- ❑ Pencil
- ❑ Access to a copy machine that enlarges
- ❑ Scissors
- ❑ Navy pillow case

1 Ask a grown-up to help you iron the transfer web to the white fabric. Again, be sure to iron on the paper side so the web becomes fused to the fabric.

2 Using tracing paper and a pencil, trace the letters of your name (or the name of a friend for whom you are making the pillow). Use the alphabet on pages 188.

3 Repeat Steps 3, 4, 5, 6, and 7 from **Red Wish**.

GREEN NIGHT NOTE

CHECK LIST

- ❏ ½ yard yellow fabric
- ❏ 1 yard iron-on, paper-backed transfer web
- ❏ Iron
- ❏ Tracing paper
- ❏ Pencil
- ❏ Access to a copy machine that enlarges
- ❏ Scissors
- ❏ Green pillow case

1 Ask a grown-up to help you iron the transfer web to the yellow fabric.

2 Using tracing paper and a pencil, trace the letters for "Sweet Dreams." Use the alphabet on pages 188.

3 Repeat Steps 3, 4, 5, 6, and 7 from **Red Wish**.

You worked hard! Wrap a colorful case around a fluffy pillow and take a nap.

CARROT

Keep Out of the Carrot Patch

Sneaky Veggie Eaters

Sneaky Veggie Eaters

Give these critters as a gift for someone's kitchen or gardening shed. If you feel industrious, you can plant some of the seeds and have veggies at harvest time.

CHECK LIST

- ❑ 10-inch square of orange fabric
- ❑ Pencil
- ❑ Compass
- ❑ Tracing paper
- ❑ Clear tape
- ❑ Carbon paper
- ❑ Black fine-tip permanent marker
- ❑ 4 cotton balls
- ❑ Thin white cloth-covered craft wire
- ❑ Tacky glue
- ❑ 8½-inch-long wood stick
- ❑ Straight pins
- ❑ 10-inch square of blue/white checked fabric
- ❑ Scissors
- ❑ 10-inch square of brown fabric
- ❑ 10-inch square of paper-backed transfer web
- ❑ Iron
- ❑ Pinking shears
- ❑ ½ yard of 3-inch-wide dark green paper ribbon
- ❑ White drawing paper
- ❑ Colored pencils: orange, green
- ❑ 4-inch-long wood stick
- ❑ Large pumpkin seed packet
- ❑ Spanish moss
- ❑ ½ yard of ⅛-inch-wide green satin ribbon

FARMER PETE SCARECROW

MAKE FACE

1 Place the point of the compass in the center of the orange fabric, set the compass for 4 inches, and draw a circle. The circle will be an 8-inch circle. Cut out the circle.

2 Using tracing paper and a pencil, trace the scarecrow face pattern on page 68.

3 Tape a small piece of carbon paper to the orange fabric circle. Place the traced pattern over the carbon paper, positioning it so the mouth is about 2½ inches from the circle's edge. Outline the face again. The carbon paper will transfer the face to the fabric.

4 Outline the face and color the eyes and nose with the black marker.

5 Position the circle in your hand with the face against your palm. Place 3 or 4 cotton balls in the center. Pull the edges of the circle tightly around the cotton.

6 Adjust the fabric and cotton balls so the face is centered on the front. Twist a piece of craft wire once around the fabric to hold the cotton in place.

DRESS SCARECROW

1 Put glue on 1 end of the long stick and insert it through the opening between the gathers in the bottom of the orange fabric head and into the cotton.

2 Twist the craft wire more tightly to secure the cotton ball and stick.

3 Using tracing paper and a pencil, trace the neck scarf pattern on page 69.

4 Pin the pattern to the blue/white checked fabric and cut out 1 scarf.

5 Tie the scarf around the neck of the scarecrow, covering the white craft wire.

6 Fold the square of brown fabric in half and cut along the fold.

7 Ask a grown-up to help you iron the transfer web between the 2 pieces of brown fabric.

8 Using tracing paper and a pencil, trace hat and brim patterns on page 69.

9 Pin the patterns to the brown fabric and cut out 1 hat and 1 brim.

10 Roll the hat piece into a cone shape, overlap the ends, and glue to hold it together. Use pinking shears to clip off the top of the cone.

11 Glue the hat to the top of the scarecrow's head.

12 Pull the brim piece over the hat piece and glue at the seam.

13 Fold the top of the hat down and make a crease with your fingers to secure the fold.

MAKE GRASS & SIGN

1 To make the grass, cut the paper ribbon into 5 pieces, each measuring 2 inches long.

2 Cut thin vertical strips down from the long edge of each piece of ribbon to about ½ inch from the bottom of the strip. Look at Diagram A to see what to do.

Diagram A

3 Using tracing paper and a pencil, trace the pumpkin patch sign pattern.

4 Tape carbon paper to the drawing paper and tape the traced sign pattern over the carbon paper. Outline the pattern again. The carbon paper will transfer the pattern to the drawing paper.

5 Outline the lettering and pumpkins with the black marker.

6 Use orange and green pencils to color the pumpkins.

7 Glue the sign to the short stick.

ASSEMBLE & GLUE

1 Open the seed packet but leave the seeds inside.

2 Put glue on the bottom of the long stick and insert the stick into the seed packet. Angle the stick toward the right bottom corner of the packet, letting the scarecrow rest in the top left corner.

3 Glue the scarecrow stick to the inside front cover of the seed packet and glue the sign stick to the top part of the inside front cover. Look at the photograph to see how to position the sticks.

4 Glue the Spanish moss and the grass pieces to the inside front cover of the seed packet. Look at the photograph to see how this should look.

5 Glue the back cover of the packet to all to secure everything in place in the seed packet.

6 To make the hanger, cut a 10-inch piece of green satin ribbon. Find the center of the ribbon and make a 2-inch loop at the center.

7 Tie a knot at the bottom of the loop, leaving 3-inch tails. Tie knots in the bottoms of the tails. Look at Diagram B to see what to do.

8 Glue the knots to the back near the top of the seed packet.

Diagram B

SCARECROW FACE

PUMPKIN PATCH SIGN

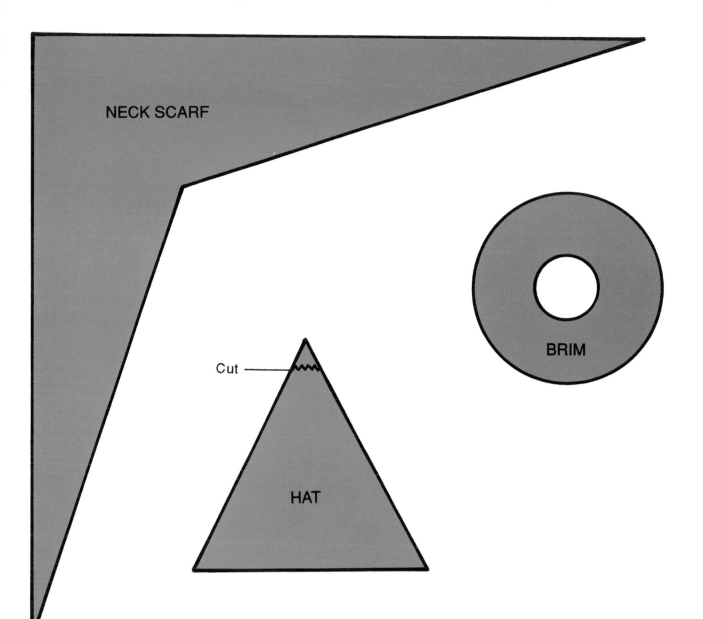

NECK SCARF

Cut

HAT

BRIM

CORNY PORKER

MAKE FACE

1 Repeat all "Make Face" steps of **Farmer Pete Scarecrow**, but this time, use pink fabric and trace the pig face pattern on page 71.

DRESS PIG

1 Repeat the "Make Dress" Steps 1, 2, and 3 of **Farmer Pete Scarecrow**.

2 Pin the scarf pattern to the black/red checked fabric and cut out 1 scarf.

3 Tie the scarf around the neck of the pig, covering the white craft wire.

4 Using tracing paper and a pencil, trace the pig ear pattern on page 71 and cut out.

5 Pin the pattern to the pink felt and use pinking shears to cut out 2 ears.

6 Glue 1 point of the ear to the back of the pig's head on the left side. Fold the other point down in front and glue. Repeat with the second ear, gluing it to the back on the right side. Look at the photograph to see how the pig ears should look.

MAKE GRASS & SIGN

1 Repeat "Make Grass & Sign" Steps 1, 2, 3, and 4 of **Farmer Pete Scarecrow**, but this time, trace the corn patch sign.

2 Outline the lettering and the corn with the black marker.

3 Use yellow and green pencils to color the corn.

4 Glue the sign to the short stick.

ASSEMBLE & GLUE

1 Repeat all "Assemble & Glue" steps of **Farmer Pete Scarecrow**, but this time, place the pig stick in the corn packet.

PIG FACE

PIG EAR

CORN PATCH SIGN

HUNGRY MUNCH RABBIT

MAKE FACE

1 Repeat all "Make Face" steps of **Farmer Pete Scarecrow**, but this time use the beige fabric and trace the rabbit face on page 73.

DRESS RABBIT

1 Repeat "Make Dress" Steps 1, 2, and 3 of **Farmer Pete Scarecrow**.

2 Pin the scarf pattern to the red/white checked fabric and cut out 1 scarf.

3 Tie the fabric around the neck of the rabbit, covering the white craft wire.

4 Using tracing paper and a pencil, trace the rabbit ear pattern on page 73.

5 Pin the pattern to the beige felt and use pinking shears to cut out 2 ears.

6 Use the paintbrush to paint the center of each ear pink. Let the paint dry.

7 Glue the bottom points of the ears to the center back of the rabbit's head. Fold down the top of the left ear and glue. Look at the photograph to see how the rabbit should look.

8 With your finger, lightly dab some pink paint onto the rabbit's cheeks.

MAKE GRASS & SIGN

1 Repeat "Grass & Sign" Steps 1, 2, and 3 of **Farmer Pete Scarecrow**, but this time, trace the carrot patch sign.

2 Outline the lettering and carrots with the black marker.

3 Use orange and green pencils to color the carrots.

4 Glue the sign to the short stick.

ASSEMBLE & GLUE

1 Repeat all "Assemble & Glue" steps of **Farmer Pete Scarecrow**, but this time, place the rabbit stick in the carrot packet.

Vegetables are good for you and now you have 3 friends who like them, too!

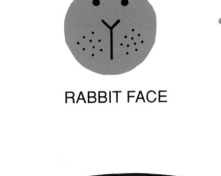

RABBIT FACE

RABBIT EAR

CARROT PATCH SIGN

Spittin' Watermelon Seeds

Spittin' Watermelon Seeds

Watermelons bring ideas of summer fun. Brighten even winter days by wearing a watermelon-decorated shirt that you have made.

Ask a grown-up to help you purchase some of the check-list items. Also ask a grown-up to help you use the craft knife.

STAMPED SHIRT

CHECK LIST

- ❑ 5 watermelon wood cutouts (if you buy these, you do not need the next 5 items)
- ❑ Tracing paper
- ❑ Pencil
- ❑ Carbon paper
- ❑ Clear tape
- ❑ 20-inch by 4-inch piece of balsa wood
- ❑ Craft knife
- ❑ Ruler
- ❑ Moleskin with adhesive backing
- ❑ Fabric paints: orange, green, purple, blue, red, yellow, pink
- ❑ Paintbrushes
- ❑ White T-shirt or sweatshirt
- ❑ Fabric glue
- ❑ Faux rhinestones: 5 moons, 6 stars, 2 hearts

TRACE & CUT

1 If you have purchased the watermelon wood cutouts, skip to Step 4. If you did not purchase them, then trace a watermelon pattern from page 77 and cut it out, cutting the rind from the melon.

2 Place the melon and rind patterns on top of carbon paper that is placed on the balsa wood with dark side touching the wood. Retrace the outline, allowing the carbon paper to transfer the pattern to the balsa wood. Trace both patterns 5 times.

3 Then, ask a grown-up to help you use a craft knife to cut out the 5 melon and rind cutouts from the balsa wood.

4 Use a ruler to mark a 5-inch square on moleskin. Then, cut out the square.

5 Take the paper backing off the moleskin and stick a melon and a rind cutout to the moleskin, leaving a space between each pattern to cut between the wood shapes. Trim the moleskin close to the melon and rind.

6 Repeat Steps 4 and 5, using more moleskin and the other 4 melon and rind wood shapes.

PAINT & STAMP

1 Take the white T-shirt or sweatshirt and decide where you want to position the melons and rinds.

2 Paint the moleskin of the cutouts the colors you would like.

3 Use 1 watermelon shape like a stamp and push it down on the shirt. The painted shape will be transferred to the shirt.

4 Do the same with the rind shape, positioning it under the watermelon shape, leaving about ⅛ inch of white space between. Let the paint dry.

5 Repeat Steps 3 and 4 with the remaining watermelon and rind moleskin stamps. Remember to work fairly quickly so that the paint does not dry before you stamp it on the shirt.

6 Glue the faux rhinestones to the melon any way you would like. Look at the photograph to see how this might look.

WATERMELON

RIND

STENCILLED SHIRT

TRACE & GLUE

CHECK LIST

❑ Tracing paper
❑ Pencil
❑ Carbon paper
❑ Clear tape
❑ Manila folder
❑ Ruler
❑ Craft knife
❑ Fabric paints: orange, green, purple, blue, red, yellow, pink
❑ Paintbrush or sponge
❑ White T-shirt or sweatshirt
❑ Fabric glue
❑ Multi-colored plastic confetti

1 Using tracing paper and a pencil, trace the watermelon and rind patterns on page 77 and cut them out.

2 Place carbon paper over the manila folder with carbon side against the folder.

3 Place the patterns on top of the carbon paper and retrace the outline. The carbon paper will transfer the patterns to the manila folder.

4 Use a ruler to draw a square about 1 inch from the edges of the patterns.

5 Ask a grown-up to help you use a craft knife to cut out the square and then to cut out the watermelon and rind patterns. You now have a watermelon and rind stencil.

PAINT & GLUE

1 Take a light colored T-shirt or sweatshirt and decide where you want to position the watermelons and the rinds.

2 Place the watermelon stencil on the shirt where desired. Then, use a paintbrush or sponge and the color paints you'd like to paint the watermelon shape onto the shirt. Let the paint dry.

3 Repeat Step 2 to paint as many watermelons as you want on the shirt.

4 Place the rind stencil on the shirt next to a painted watermelon and paint the rind. Repeat next to each painted watermelon.

5 After all the paint is dry, glue plastic confetti to the melon to look like seeds. Look at the photograph to see how this might look.

■ ■ ■ ■ ■ ■ ■ ■ ■ ■ ■ ■ ■ ■ ■ ■ ■

Get ready to carry summer cheer with you when you wear a melon shirt.

■ ■ ■ ■ ■ ■ ■ ■ ■ ■ ■ ■ ■ ■ ■ ■ ■

Summer Wood Jewelry

Wood jewelry is popular now. Watermelons with hearts and stars can be made into a piece of jewelry that is a nice accessory to almost any outfit. Look at the photograph on page 75.

Ask a grown-up to help you purchase some of the check-list items. Also ask a grown-up to help you use the craft knife.

CHECK LIST

❑ 3¼-inch by 2-inch wood watermelon cutout
(if you do not purchase the cutout, then you can make one, using tracing paper, a pencil, carbon paper, a scrap of balsa wood, and a craft knife)
❑ ¼-inch awl
❑ 6 wood heart beads, about 1-inch wide
❑ 4 wood star beads, about 1-inch wide
❑ Acrylic paints: white, pink, blue, and any other colors you would like
❑ Paintbrushes
❑ Fine-grade sandpaper
❑ Faux rhinestones: 1 moon, 2 stars
❑ Tacky glue
❑ 1½ yards of ¹⁄₁₆-inch-wide red satin cord

CUT & PAINT

1 Use a purchased wood watermelon cutout or make one. (Trace a pattern from page 77, and cut it out. Place a piece of carbon paper on the balsa wood with the carbon side against the wood. Place the watermelon pattern over the carbon paper. Retrace the pattern. The carbon paper will transfer it to the wood. Ask a grown-up to help you use a craft knife to cut 1 watermelon from the wood.)

2 Ask a grown-up to help you use the awl to make a small hole at each top corner of the watermelon cutout.

3 Paint the watermelon cutout white. Let the paint dry.

4 Then, paint the watermelon pink with a blue rind. Leave a strip of white between the 2 colors on the cutout. Look at the photograph to see how this should look. Let the paint dry.

5 Paint the heart and star beads in any colors you would like. Let the paint dry.

SAND & GLUE

1 Use the sandpaper to sand some of the color off, letting the white show through. This makes the watermelon cutout look worn.

2 Glue the faux rhinestones to the painted watermelon cutout.

CUT & TIE

1 Cut the red cord into 2 pieces, each 13½ inches long.

2 Tie a knot in 1 end of 1 piece of the cord and pull the other end through 1 corner of the pink watermelon. String 1 heart, 1 star, 1 heart, 1 star and 1 heart.

3 Repeat Step 2 above, pulling the second piece of red cord through the other corner of the watermelon. Again, string the hearts and stars alternately.

4 Tie the ends of the strings together, near their ends, to make a necklace.

Dress up and show off your watermelon necklace. It'll be 1-of-a-kind, and it's all yours!

NOTE: You can make other watermelon necklaces. Purchase (or make) watermelon cutouts, punch small holes in the corners, and paint them white. Then, paint the watermelons any colors you would like (purple with a green rind is one suggestion) and sand them when the paint is dry. Then, glue multi-colored plastic confetti or faux rhinestones to the watermelon. Use different colored satin cord (for example, yellow for a purple watermelon) and string different colored hearts, stars, or other shapes on the cord to make another unique necklace.

Miss Molly Dolly

What a versatile companion! Your Molly Dolly can move her arms and legs and provide a happy smile to decorate your favorite room in the house.

Ask a grown-up to help you purchase some of the check-list items.

CHECK LIST

- ❏ Watercolor paper
- ❏ Spray bottle filled with water
- ❏ Watercolor paints: blue, purple, blue-green, brown, yellow, pink
- ❏ Tracing paper
- ❏ Pencil
- ❏ Carbon paper
- ❏ 4 brass paper fasteners
- ❏ Black fine-tip permanent marker
- ❏ Crayons: blue, red
- ❏ Tacky glue

PAINT & TRACE

1 Lightly spray the watercolor paper with water.

2 Paint most of the paper with blue, purple, and blue-green, letting the colors overlap and blend. Let the paint dry.

3 Paint a yellow and green area on part of the paper, a brown and green area on another part, and a pink area on another part of the paper. Let all of the paint dry.

4 Using tracing paper and a pencil, trace all of the patterns on pages 84 and 85.

5 Tape some carbon paper to the water-color paper with the carbon side down.

TRANSFER & COLOR

1 Tape the patterns over the carbon paper. Arrange them so the patterns of the body, the skirt, and 2 sleeves are over the blue/purple area of the watercolor paper, the patterns for the belt and for 2 arms over the yellow/green area, the hair piece over the brown/green area, and the head and 2 legs over the pink area.

2 Trace around the patterns again. The carbon paper will transfer the shapes to the watercolor paper.

3 Using tracing paper and a pencil, trace the face pattern. Use the carbon paper to transfer it to the head part.

4 Use a black marker to outline the eyes, nose, and mouth.

5 Use crayons to color the eyes blue and the mouth red.

CUT & GLUE

1 Cut out all of the patterns.

2 Using the end of a pin, nail, or paper fastener, punch small holes in the watercolor paper shapes, according to the marks on the patterns.

3 Glue the hair to the head, the head to the neck, the sleeves to the tops of the arms, the skirt to the middle part of the body, and the belt over the skirt.

4 Use the paper fasteners to hook the arms and legs to the body.

● ● ● ● ● ● ● ● ● ● ● ● ● ●

Remember to take your paper doll to your next play time with friends. She'll be a hit!

● ● ● ● ● ● ● ● ● ● ● ● ● ●

SKIRT

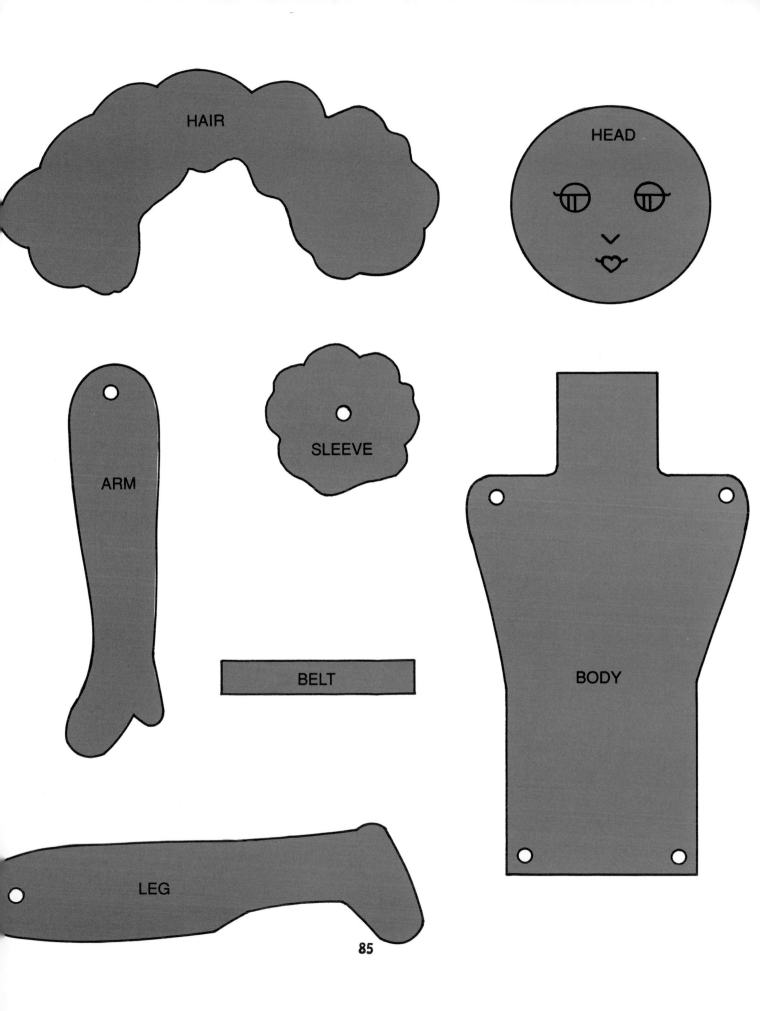

HAIR

HEAD

ARM

SLEEVE

BELT

BODY

LEG

Happy Flowers Box

Learn a new painting technique and use it to give a box a special look.

Ask a grown-up to help you purchase some of the items. Also ask a grown-up to help you use the craft knife.

CHECK LIST

❑ 5-inch by 2½-inch wood box with lid
❑ Facial Tissue
❑ Acrylic paints: yellow, white, blue
❑ Paint sponges
❑ Tracing paper
❑ Pencil
❑ Carbon paper
❑ Clear tape
❑ Manila folder
❑ Craft knife
❑ Masking tape

1 Using a sponge, paint the box and lid yellow. Let the paint dry.

2 Tear the tissue into tiny pieces. Using a clean sponge, dab white paint onto the box and lid, mixing the tissue pieces with the paint. Let the paint dry. The tissue pieces give the box a textured look.

3 Using tracing paper and a pencil, trace the flower pattern.

4 Tape a piece of carbon paper onto the manila folder with the carbon side against the folder. Place the flower pattern over the carbon paper and retrace the pattern.

5 Ask a grown-up to help you use a craft knife to cut around the flower pattern so that you have a solid shape.

6 Place the manila folder flower shape on the painted wood box lid. Hold it in place and, using a sponge, paint blue around the shape. You will now have the outline of the flower on the lid.

7 Repeat Step 6 several times, outlining the flower on the lid and the box. Let the paint dry.

■●★ ■●★ ■●★ ■●★ ■

Your cheerful flower box now has a spirited spring look.

■●★ ■●★ ■●★ ■●★ ■

FLOWER

Nice To Meet You

Meeting people is fun. With this necklace, the new friends you meet will know your name right from the beginning and you won't have to remind them.

Ask a grown-up to help you purchase some of the check-list items. Also ask a grown-up to help you use the drill.

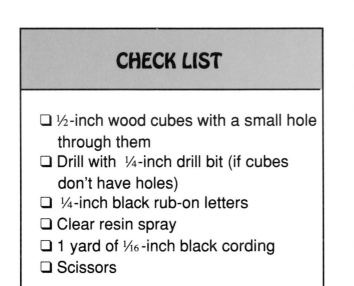

CHECK LIST

- ❑ ½-inch wood cubes with a small hole through them
- ❑ Drill with ¼-inch drill bit (if cubes don't have holes)
- ❑ ¼-inch black rub-on letters
- ❑ Clear resin spray
- ❑ 1 yard of ¹⁄₁₆-inch black cording
- ❑ Scissors

COUNT & SPELL

1 Count the number of letters in the name or names you want to spell for 1 necklace. Add 1 cube for every space between the names. The total count is the number of wood cubes you need.

2 If the wood cubes you purchased do not have a hole through them, ask a grown-up to drill a small hole through each cube.

3 On the 4 sides of the cube that do not have holes, rub the first letter of the name onto each surface.

4 Repeat Step 3 with the remaining cubes and letters of the name. If you are spelling 2 names, remember to leave a blank cube between the names.

SPRAY & STRING

1 Spray the cubes with clear resin. Let the resin dry.

2 Cut the cording to the length you want for the necklace.

3 String the cubes onto the cording. Tie the ends into a knot.

Wear this necklace with pride. It's what you made and who you are!

Sunny Flower Pin

Would you believe fresh flowers growing on your dress, shirt or sweater?
This pin looks too real to be true. Look at the photograph on page 90.

Ask a grown-up to help you purchase some of the check-list items. Also ask a grown-up to help you use the wire cutters and hot glue gun.

CHECK LIST

- ❏ 2½-inch square of brown woven fabric
- ❏ 1½-inch covered button set with teeth
- ❏ Scissors
- ❏ Wire cutters
- ❏ ½ yard of 3-inch-wide yellow paper twist
- ❏ Tracing paper
- ❏ Pencil
- ❏ Long tweezers
- ❏ Jewelry pin
- ❏ Hot glue gun and glue sticks

1 Cut a 2½-inch circle from the brown fabric. You might want to use a juice glass, half dollar, or other small circular object to help outline the circle.

2 Center and stretch the fabric over the button sides. Stretch and ease the fabric so it catches firmly and evenly to the teeth all around. Then, snap on the back plate of the button.

3 Ask a grown-up to help you cut off the button shank with wire cutters.

4 Using tracing paper and a pencil, trace the small, medium, and large petal patterns. Cut them out.

LARGE   MEDIUM   SMALL

5 Position the petal patterns on the yellow paper twist. Trace and cut 13 small, 12 medium, and 28 large paper twist petals.

6 Glue the petals to the back of the button in layers. Start with the smallest petals and then glue on the larger ones. Let the glue dry.

7 With the long tweezers, roll the ends of the paper petals to get the curl.

8 Glue the jewelry pin to the button back.

Now a bit of sun can brighten your dress or sweater.

> **NOTE:** You can also glue the flower onto a barrette clasp, instead of a pin, and wear it in your hair.

Sassy Shelf Animals

*Your bookshelf or desk can be a comfortable home
for these critters made from wood tongue depressors.*

**Ask a grown-up to help you purchase
some of the check-list items.**

PINK PIG

CHECK LIST
(For 1)

- ❑ 3 wood tongue depressors, 4 inches long
- ❑ 4-inch-long craft stick
- ❑ 14-inch by 5-inch strip of printed fabric
- ❑ 1-inch wood cube
- ❑ Acrylic paints: pink, gray
- ❑ Paintbrushes
- ❑ Scrap drawing paper
- ❑ ½ yard of ¹⁄₁₆-inch-wide pink satin ribbon
- ❑ Large-eye needle
- ❑ Tacky glue
- ❑ Ivory eyelet trim

PAINT & GLUE

1 For the pig, paint the tongue depressors, the craft stick and the cube pink. Let the paint dry.

2 With a thin paintbrush, paint the face and the hooves gray. Look at the photograph to see how this should look.

3 For the legs, glue the small end of 2 pink tongue depressors to 1 surface of the cube with the large ends of the depressors down.

4 For the head, glue the small end of the remaining tongue depressor to the opposite surface of the cube with the large end of the depressor pointing up. Glue the craft stick centered horizontally to the back of the head piece.

TEAR & STITCH

1 Tear about 2 inches from 1 long edge of the printed fabric strip. Look at Diagram A on page 94. On the opposite long edge, turn the fabric under about ¼ inch and glue the edge down to form the collar hem. Look at Diagram A again.

2 Cut pink ribbon into a 4-inch piece and 2 pieces, each measuring 7 inches.

3 Using the needle and a 7-inch ribbon piece, sew short, even stitches through the turned-under long edge for the collar. Look at Diagram B on page 94.

4 Cut ½-inch slits in fabric about ½ inch from collar where the arms need to come through the fabric. Pull the arms through the fabric.

5 Tie the ends of the pink ribbon together, gathering the collar around the neck. Make sure the short edges of the fabric meet in the back. Glue the back seam together.

6 Using the needle, thread the remaining 7-inch ribbon piece through 1 long edge of the ivory trim.

7 Wrap the trim around the neck over the collar and tie the ends in back, gathering the lace to fit the neck.

TRACE & GLUE

1 Using tracing paper and a pencil, trace the ear patterns. Cut them out. Trace around the patterns on the drawing paper. Cut out the ears.

2 Paint the ears pink. Let the paint dry. Glue the ears to the back of the head.

3 Tie the 4-inch ribbon piece into a bow. Glue to the top center of the pig's head.

These take only a few minutes to craft. Have fun and make them all.

NOTE: For the dog, repeat the steps to make the pig. Use brown paint, the dog ear patterns and a bead necklace. For the cow, repeat the steps but use white and black paints, the cow ear patterns and red ribbon. Look at the photograph to see the variations.

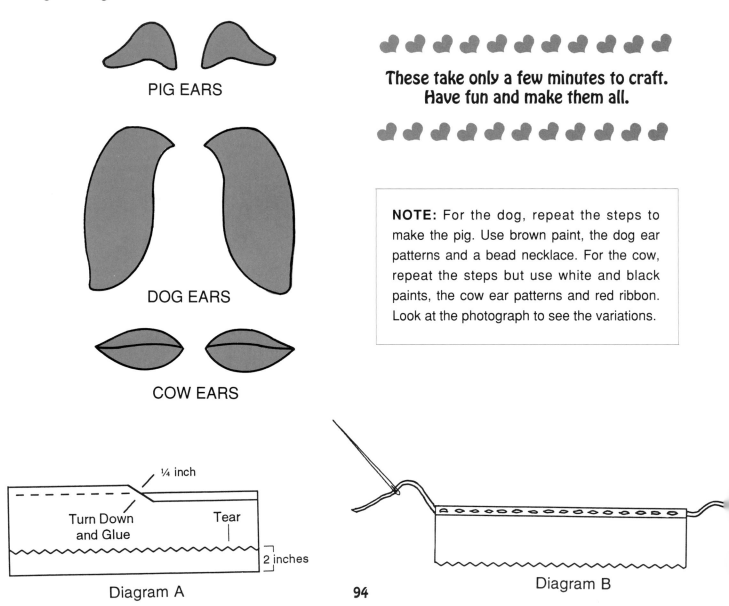

PIG EARS

DOG EARS

COW EARS

¼ inch

Turn Down and Glue

Tear

2 inches

Diagram A

94

Diagram B

Star Secret Keeper

That special place where you keep secret treasures or collect personal trinkets should be decorated just for you. Try this star box.
Look at the photograph on page 97.

Ask a grown-up to help you purchase some of the check-list items. Also ask a grown-up to help you use the craft knife.

CHECK LIST

- ❏ 9-inch by 6-inch by 5-inch wood box with molding and lid
- ❏ Black enamel paint
- ❏ Acrylic paints: red, blue, green, yellow
- ❏ Paintbrushes
- ❏ 2½-inch wood star cutout
- ❏ Manila folder
- ❏ Craft knife
- ❏ Tracing paper
- ❏ Pencil
- ❏ Scissors
- ❏ Ruler
- ❏ Masking tape
- ❏ Wood glue
- ❏ Rough sand paper
- ❏ Black narrow-point, felt-tip marker

PAINT & TRACE

1 Paint the box with black enamel paint. Wait about 2 hours.

2 Paint red acrylic paint over the black enamel. The red paint will streak with the black. That's the look you want. Let the paint dry.

3 Using tracing paper and a pencil, trace the zigzag pattern on page 96. Cut out the pattern.

4 Tape the pattern to the manila folder and trace around it.

5 Ask a grown-up to help you use the craft knife to cut the pattern from the manila folder.

6 Place a masking tape band around the 4 sides of the box, about 2 inches down from the top edge.

7 Tape the cutout pattern to the box with the straight edge near the top of the box and the zigzag part about 1 inch above the masking tape line.

8 Paint the area between the tape edge and the zigzag pattern blue. Look at the photograph to see how this should look.

9 Move the zigzag pattern over and repeat Steps 7 and 8 all around the box.

10 Tape the pattern above the bottom edge of the 4 sides of the box so the zigzag pattern is pointing down about 1 inch above the bottom edge. Paint the space below the zigzag edge blue.

11 Repeat Step 10 on the 2 long edges of the box lid.

12 Outline the zigzag border with the black felt-tip marker.

13 Paint the bottom and lid molding green. Let the paint dry.

STENCIL & PAINT

1 With tracing paper and a pencil, trace around the star cutout. Cut out the pattern.

2 Tape the star pattern to the manila folder and trace around it.

3 Draw a square box around the star tracing; the outline should be about 1 inch from the points of the star. Use scissors to cut out the box on this line.

4 Ask a grown-up to help you use the craft knife to cut out the star pattern inside the box. Now, you have a star stencil.

5 Tape the stencil to the center of the short side of the box and paint the star yellow. Repeat on the other short side.

6 Use the stencil to paint 3 yellow stars on the front and the back of the box. Look at the photograph to see how to position the stars.

PAINT & GLUE

1 Paint the wood star cutout yellow. Let the paint dry.

2 Glue the yellow star cutout to the center of the lid.

3 Use the star stencil to paint 2 yellow stars, 1 on each side of the wood star.

4 Sand the yellow stenciled stars on the box and the lid until some of the red paint shows through to make the box look old.

Your bright star box is ready to hold presents to yourself or to someone close.

ZIGZAG

96

Tic Toc Heart Clock

Time and country are close to your heart when you make this clock. Paint the wood cutout in patriotic colors and finish the clock with a simple timepiece.

Ask a grown-up to help you purchase some of the check-list items. Also ask a grown-up to help you use the drill.

CHECK LIST

- ❏ 7-inch wood heart cutout
- ❏ Compass
- ❏ Pencil
- ❏ Drill
- ❏ Ruler
- ❏ Small clock works with 2 wands
- ❏ 4 wood star cutouts
- ❏ Acrylic paints: white, red, blue, yellow
- ❏ Paintbrushes
- ❏ Tacky glue

DRAW & DRILL

1 Find the center of the heart and position the needle part of the compass there. Set the compass for 2 inches and draw a 4-inch circle on the heart front.

2 Drill a small hole in the center of the circle large enough to fit the clock works.

3 Use a ruler to measure and draw ½-inch-wide stripes on the front of the heart.

PAINT & GLUE

1 Paint the circle on the heart blue. Let the paint dry.

2 Paint every other stripe on the heart white. Let the paint dry.

3 Paint the other stripes and the edges of the heart red. Let the paint dry

4 Paint the star cutouts yellow.

5 Glue the star cutouts around the blue circle. Place them where 12, 3, 6, and 9 are on a clock. Look at the photograph to see where to place them.

6 Attach the clock works with the wands through the center hole according to the directions given with the clock.

Do you know how to tell time? If not, you can learn with your very own clock.

Show-Off Lights

A plain light switch is usually overlooked on the wall. Change that.
Create these hand-painted light switch covers to brighten the whole room.

Ask a grown-up to help you purchase some of the check-list items. Also ask a grown-up to help you use the craft knife and screwdriver.

NIGHT SCENE

CHECK LIST

❑ Round-top wood light switch cover
❑ Acrylic paints: medium blue, navy, yellow, white
❑ Narrow paintbrushes
❑ Tracing paper
❑ Pencil
❑ Carbon paper
❑ Masking tape
❑ 6-inch square of balsa wood
❑ Craft knife
❑ Wood cutouts: 1 moon, 3 stars
❑ Tacky glue
❑ Screwdriver

1 Paint the light switch cover blue. Let the paint dry.

2 Paint the moon and star cutouts yellow. Let the paint dry.

3 Using tracing paper and a pencil, trace the city pattern on page 103. Cut it out.

4 Tape the carbon paper to the balsa wood with the carbon side against the wood. Tape the city pattern over the carbon paper and retrace the pattern. The carbon paper will transfer the outline to the balsa wood.

5 Ask a grown-up to help you use the craft knife to cut the city pattern out of the balsa wood.

6 Paint the city navy. Let the paint dry.

7 Paint white dots on the city to look like lighted windows. Look at the photograph to see how this should look.

8 Glue the city, stars, and moon to the switch plate. Look at the photograph to see how to position the pieces.

9 Ask a grown-up to help you use a screwdriver to attach the light switch cover in place on the wall.

SUNNY FLOWERS

CHECK LIST

- ❑ Oval wood light switch cover
- ❑ Acrylic paints: light blue, yellow, orange, red, green, purple
- ❑ Paintbrushes
- ❑ Tracing paper
- ❑ Pencil
- ❑ Scissors
- ❑ Masking tape
- ❑ Wood cutouts: 1 circle, 3 flower tops, 3 stems
- ❑ Tacky glue
- ❑ Screwdriver

1 Paint the light switch cover light blue. Let the paint dry.

2 Paint 1 flower top red, 1 orange, and 1 purple. Paint the 3 stems green. Let the paint dry.

3 Paint the wood circle yellow. Let the paint dry.

4 Using tracing paper and a pencil, trace the sun pattern on page 103. Cut it out.

5 Tape the sun pattern to the switch cover and trace around it. Paint this area of the cover yellow. Let the paint dry.

6 Glue the yellow circle to the middle of the painted sun pattern.

7 Glue the stems and the flower tops along the bottom of the cover plate. Look at the photograph. Let the glue dry.

8 Using green paint, draw leaves at the sides of each stem.

9 Ask a grown-up to help you use a screwdriver to attach the light switch cover to the wall.

LOVABLE BEARS

CHECK LIST

- ❑ Rectangle wood light switch cover
- ❑ Acrylic paints: white, red, brown, navy
- ❑ Paintbrushes
- ❑ Wood cutouts: 4 bears, 4 hearts
- ❑ Ruler
- ❑ Pencil
- ❑ Tacky glue
- ❑ Screwdriver

1 Paint the light switch cover white. Let the paint dry.

2 Paint the border of the light switch cover and the heart cutouts red. Let the paint dry.

3 Paint the bear cutouts brown. Let the paint dry.

4 Use a ruler and pencil and draw lines down the cover every ½ inch. Then, draw lines across the cover every ½ inch. You will have small squares all over the cover. Press lightly with the pencil so the lines are not too dark.

5 Paint every other square navy so you have a navy-and-white checked pattern. Let the paint dry.

6 Glue the hearts and the bears to the cover. Look at the photograph for an idea of how to place the cutouts.

7 Ask a grown-up to help you use a screwdriver to attach the light switch cover to the wall.

♥♥♥♥♥♥♥♥♥♥♥

These light switch covers now really show off your room. Use your imagination to decorate other covers.

♥♥♥♥♥♥♥♥♥♥♥

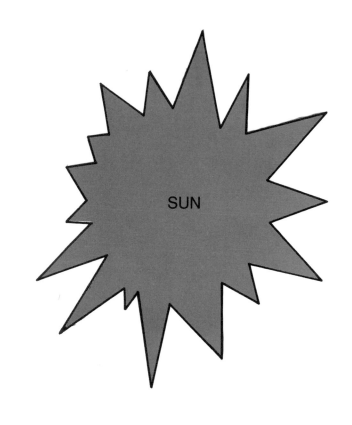

SUN

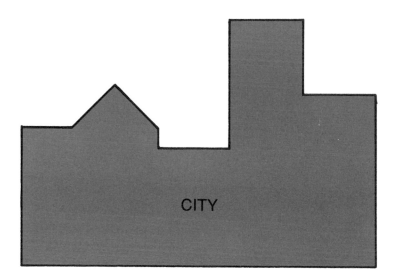

CITY

Color Plush Pillows

Color Plush Pillows

Your imagination will help you think of patterns to decorate comfortable pillows with fabric markers. Or follow the ideas shown in the photograph.

Ask a grown-up to help you purchase some of the check-list items. Also ask a grown-up to help you use the iron.

CHECK LIST

❑ White pillow with zip-on cover
❑ Dressmaker's pen
❑ Tracing paper
❑ Embroidery transfer pencil
❑ Iron
❑ Cardboard
❑ Fabric markers: multi-color pack

TRACE & IRON

1 Unzip the pillow cover and take the pillow from the cover. (If you cannot find a covered pillow form, purchase a throw pillow. Clip some threads at the seam and remove the stuffing so the fabric will lie flat.)

2 Decide on the picture you want on your pillow. Draw the outline on the pillow cover with a dressmaker's pen. Or, select a picture from any book. Then, using tracing paper and a transfer pencil, trace the pattern.

3 Turn the tracing pencil-side down on your pillow cover and ask a grown-up to help you iron the transfer pattern onto it.

COLOR & REASSEMBLE

1 Place a piece of cardboard or heavy paper between the layers of the pillow cover so the markers will not bleed through when you color the design.

2 Color the design with markers any way you would like. Let the markers dry.

3 Replace the form in the cover and zip closed. (Or replace the stuffing and ask a grown-up to help stitch the opening closed.)

Toss a set of these on a couch, chair, or bed. They'll provide cushy comfort.

Wear-A-Medallion

Sometimes medallions you receive for good work at school or in sports gather dust on a shelf. Not these medals! You wear them for everyone to admire. Look at the photograph on page 108.

Ask a grown-up to help you purchase some of the check-list items. Also ask a grown-up to help you use the hot glue gun.

GLORIOUS GOLD

CHECK LIST

- ❏ ½ yard of 1-inch-wide gold-trimmed black satin ribbon
- ❏ ½ yard of 2½-inch-wide black satin ribbon
- ❏ ¼ yard of 1-inch-wide gold patterned black ribbon
- ❏ 4 gold seed beads
- ❏ Ruler
- ❏ Scissors
- ❏ Medium gold-colored round medallion
- ❏ Jewelry pin
- ❏ Hot glue gun and glue sticks

1 Cut a 3-inch piece and a 5-inch piece of the plain black satin ribbon.

2 Cut a 3-inch piece and a 6-inch piece of the gold-patterned ribbon.

3 Fold the longer piece of black ribbon in half and fold the shorter piece of gold-patterned ribbon in half.

4 Glue the gold-patterned ribbon to the front center of the folded black ribbon.

5 Fold lengthwise and crease the sides of the black ribbon over the edges of the gold-patterned ribbon. Look at Diagram A. Bring to a point and glue. The top ribbon is now made.

Diagram A

VOLUME LIV, ISSUE 1

H SCHOO

PRI

...mecoming a
great success

Reneé S...

The week of Septe... ...en HIgh's
100 year Homecoming. It a... ...th at 8:00
...class work... ...decorations

...the halls were
...k wa... ...ed with lunch activities
...lling sa... ...iches. Then Tuesday.
On Wed...sday the sophomores
...hmen p...ayed twister.
...tivitie... there were lots of great
...ther... ...as a night rally starting
...fabulous fireworks. Then
...th an outdoor assembly.
...came in first place
...d with 67 points,
...for third place, and the
...th 42 points.
...otball team beat Sky
...he game. Finally, the week
...mecoming Dance. The theme
...ing I Do, I Do It for You."

...d activities

Tiger
starts w

Marcu...
After a disappointin...
ball team had something to p...
with the record of two wins...
The OHS Tigers firs...
ing game against the Skyvie...
the Bobcats by a score of 34...
Brandon Parker ge...
touchdowns. Also scoring t...
were Brandon Fries and Marc...
four extra field goal points, a...
goals to bring the Tigers a w...
Ryan White passed...
help of Brandon Parker's rec...
beat this team, and this ga...
Carpenter said. "Our team h...
what we hope will be a good s...

...ek to stop Ogden

No lyin —
Tigers and
Bears both
win, oh my

...Y JEFF SIMON
...andard-Examiner staff

...MURRAY — All Coach Phil Russell
...anted toward the end of the Region 5
...ason was to get his Ogden High girls bas-
...tball team into the State 3-A Tourna-
...ent.
...The Tigers barely did, going into the
...urnament as the region's No. 5 seed. But
...n Wednesday, they pulled off the upset of

...-A GIRLS TOURNAMENT

...e tournament, knocking off Region 6
...hampion Murray High — host of the en-
...re tournament — 50-49.
...In other first-round action involving ar-

6 Fold the shorter piece of black ribbon in half lengthwise with long edges meeting in back. Glue along the line where the edges meet.

7 Pull the ribbon through the medallion loop, letting the medal rest in the middle. Look at Diagram B.

8 Make the short ribbon ends meet and glue a short end over the bottom front of the top ribbon piece. Glue the other short end over the bottom back of the top ribbon piece. Look at Diagram B again.

9 Glue the other piece of gold-patterned ribbon around the middle of the top ribbon piece to cover the raw edges. Look at Diagram C.

10 Glue the seed beads in a vertical line just above the medal on the left side. Look at Diagram C again.

11 Cut a 13-inch piece of the gold-trimmed black ribbon.

12 Tie the gold-trimmed black ribbon into a bow and cut the ends of the bow tails at an angle.

13 Glue the bow to the center back of the ribbon medal.

14 Glue the jewelry pin to the center back of the ribbons.

Diagram B

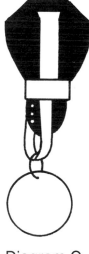

Diagram C

BRASS CIRCLE

1 Cut a 10-inch piece of the ivory crinkle ribbon. Glue the short edges together to form a circle.

2 Gather the inside long edge together with your fingers and glue in the center to complete a ribbon circle.

3 Cut a 5-inch piece of organdy ribbon.

4 Fold the organdy ribbon in half lengthwise and pull 1 end through the medallion loop, letting the medal rest in the center. Look at Diagram B on page 109.

5 Make the short ribbon ends meet and glue the ends to the middle back of the ivory crinkle ribbon circle.

6 Cut a 12-inch piece of the gold-trimmed ivory wired ribbon.

7 Make 2 loops with the ivory wired ribbon. Twist in the middle, catching the short ends. Glue to the center back of the ivory crinkle ribbon circle.

8 Cut a 10-inch piece and a 2-inch piece from the ivory-trimmed gold ribbon.

9 Cut the ends of the long piece of ivory-trimmed gold ribbon at an angle. Fold the ribbon in half, making a narrow upside-down V with tails.

10 Glue the fold of the ribbon to the center back of the ribbon circle, letting the ivory-trimmed gold ribbon tails hang.

11 Fold the small piece of ivory-trimmed gold ribbon in thirds, with the 2 ends meeting at back and glue. Glue this small ribbon square to the center front of the ivory crinkle circle. Look at the photograph to see how this should look.

12 Cut an 8-inch piece of the gold-trimmed ivory ribbon. Cut V shapes in the ends of the ribbon.

13 Fold the ribbon in half, making a wide upside-down V with tails. Glue the fold to the center back of the ribbon circle, letting the gold-trimmed ivory ribbon tails hang down.

14 Cut a 6-inch piece of the gold-striped ribbon. Cut W shapes in the ribbon ends.

15 Fold the ribbon in half, making a very wide upside-down V. Glue the fold to the back center of the ribbon circle, letting the gold-striped ribbon tails hang at an angle to the sides.

16 Glue the jewelry pin to the center back of the ribbons.

COPPER BOW

CHECK LIST

❑ 4-inch by 7-inch piece of red/black plaid fabric
❑ 7-inch square of red satin fabric
❑ Pinking shears
❑ ¼ yard of ½-inch-wide black satin ribbon
❑ Scissors
❑ Medium copper-colored medallion
❑ Jewelry pin
❑ Hot glue gun and glue sticks

1 With pinking shears, cut a rectangle, about 3-inches by 6-inches, from the plaid fabric. Also cut a square, 6 inches on each side, from the red fabric.

2 Fold the plaid rectangle in half, making the short edges meet. Place the fold at the top and position the folded rectangle in the center of the red square.

3 Handling the 2 fabrics as 1, gather the center together with your fingers. Look at Diagram D.

Diagram D

4 Tie the black ribbon around the middle, making a tight knot in the back and leaving 4-inch-long tails.

5 Cut 1 tail short. Pull the remaining ribbon tail through the medallion loop. Bring the edge of the ribbon tail to the back of the red satin bow and glue.

6 Glue the jewelry pin to the back.

■■■■■■■■■■■■■■
Dress up and wear your new pin. It's good to show off your accomplishments.
■■■■■■■■■■■■■■

"Eggs" tra Special Folks

*Take a simple wood egg and paint a gentle face and a colorful dress—
and you have an "eggs"tra special friend.*

Ask a grown-up to help you purchase some of the check-list items.

CHECK LIST

- ❏ Wood egg, 5½-inches tall
- ❏ Measuring tape
- ❏ Pencil
- ❏ Tracing paper
- ❏ Carbon paper
- ❏ Masking tape
- ❏ Acrylic paints in assorted colors
- ❏ Paintbrushes

MARK & TRACE

1 Select the front of the egg. Measure and mark according to Diagram A on page 114. Draw an arch to connect marks.

2 Find the center back of the egg. Measure and mark according to Diagram B on page 114. Connect the back line to the front line with an upside-down arch.

3 Using tracing paper and a pencil, trace the face, bow, and arm from 1 of the egg people patterns on page 114.

4 Tape the carbon paper to the egg, with the carbon side touching the egg.

5 Tape the traced pattern over the carbon paper, centering the bow at the hood line and retrace the patterns. The carbon paper will transfer the designs.

PAINT

1 Paint the hood and dress any color you would like. Look at the photograph to see what colors to use. Let the paint dry.

2 Paint the face, bow, arms, and hands any way you would like. Again, look at the photograph. Let the paint dry.

3 Paint the hair and facial features, the lines on the sleeves, the dots on the hood, and the flowers and stems any color you would like. Let the paint dry.

4 Decorate the dress any way you would like, perhaps with stripes or dots.

Don't let these endearing, hand-painted friends fall off the shelf.

NOTE: To make more "Eggs"tra Special Folks, purchase more wood eggs. Look at the photograph and follow the same directions, but use the other patterns and any colors you would like.

EGGSTRA SPECIAL FOLKS

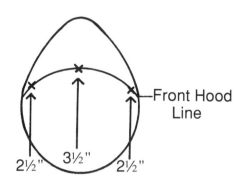

Front Hood
Line

2½"   3½"   2½"

Diagram A

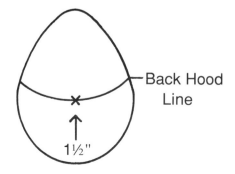

Back Hood
Line

1½"

Diagram B

Big Boo Bag

A plain white pillow case will do the job when you need a trick-or-treat bag on Halloween. But wouldn't you rather have a bright bag that can hold a lot of treats? Look at the photograph on page 116.

Ask a grown-up to help you purchase some of the check-list items. Also ask a grown-up to help you use the iron.

CHECK LIST

- ❑ Orange pillow case
- ❑ ¼ yard blue fabric
- ❑ ¼ yard black fabric
- ❑ Tracing paper
- ❑ Pencil
- ❑ Scissors
- ❑ ½ yard double-sided, paper-backed transfer web
- ❑ Access to a copy machine that enlarges
- ❑ Iron

1 Ask a grown-up to help you iron the transfer web to the black and to the blue fabrics. Iron the paper surface to fuse the transfer web to each fabric piece.

2 Using tracing paper and a pencil, trace the patterns for the star, moon, and exclamation mark on page 117. Also trace the letters B and O from the alphabet on page 188.

3 Using a copy machine, enlarge the letters so each is 4 inches high.

4 Cut the letters from the copy paper. Also cut the star, moon, and exclamation mark from the tracing paper.

5 Place the cutout star and moon shapes on the paper side of the transfer web on the blue fabric. Trace 9 stars and 4 moons.

6 Place the letters on the paper side of the transfer web on the black fabric, (the B should be backwards). Trace 1 B, 2 Os, and the exclamation mark.

7 Cut out the shapes and the letters. Remove the paper.

8 Ask a grown-up to help iron the shapes and letters onto the orange pillow case. Look at the photograph to see how to place the designs.

Hoist this bright bag over your shoulder and get ready to collect some treats.

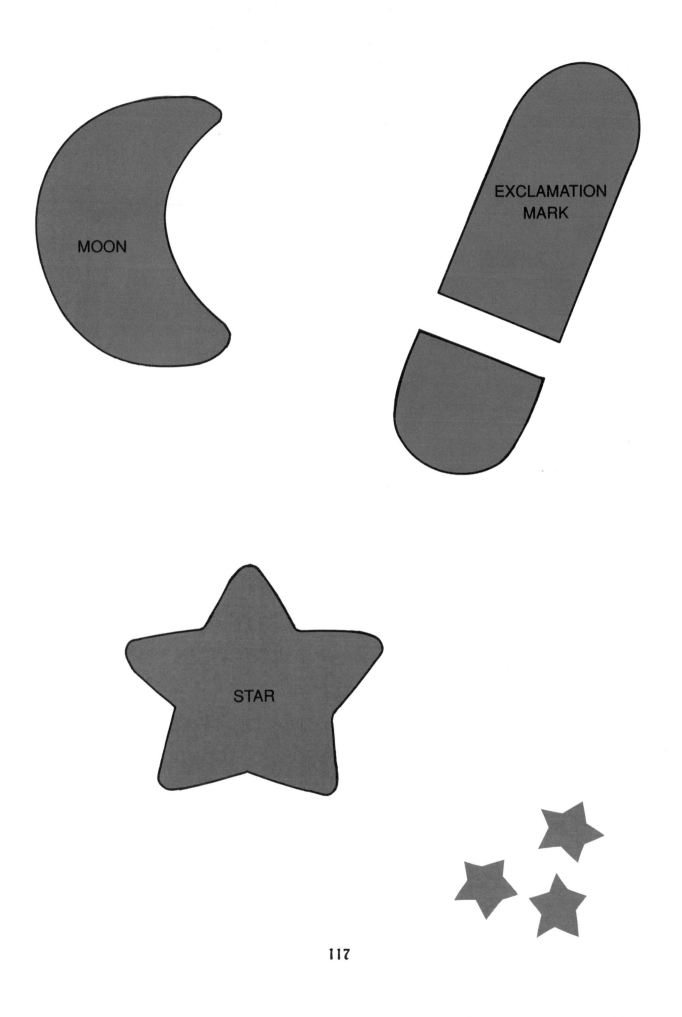

MOON

EXCLAMATION
MARK

STAR

Kooky Pumpkin Head

This pumpkin head is easy-to-make and a real treat for Halloween.
It is a great way to collect all your candy and get noticed in the dark.

Ask a grown-up to help you purchase some of the check-list items.

CHECK LIST

- ❑ Empty paint can with lid
- ❑ White metal primer spray paint
- ❑ Orange enamel spray paint
- ❑ Newspaper
- ❑ Tracing paper
- ❑ Pencil
- ❑ Masking tape
- ❑ Scissors
- ❑ 3-inch wide purple vinyl tape
- ❑ Small pinecone
- ❑ Large green silk leaf
- ❑ Clear spray resin
- ❑ Tacky glue

PRIME & PAINT

1 Purchase an empty paint can with a lid from the paint store. Do not use a can that has had paint in it. Your pumpkin head will be used to hold Halloween treats and must be clean.

2 Put some newspaper on the sidewalk or grass outside. Place the can and the lid on the newspaper.

3 Spray the outside of the can and lid with the white metal primer paint. Let the primer dry.

4 Spray the can and lid with the orange paint. Let the paint dry.

TRACE & CUT

1 Use tracing paper and a pencil to trace the moon eye, star eye, nose, and mouth patterns on page 121.

2 Tape the traced patterns to the purple vinyl tape.

3 Cut out the shapes. Now, you have the 4 face parts for the pumpkin.

119

SPRAY & GLUE

1 Spray the can and lid with clear resin. Let the resin dry.

2 Stick the eyes, nose, and mouth to the can. Look at the photograph to get an idea of where to place the pieces for the face.

3 Spray another coat of resin on the can and lid. Let the resin dry.

4 Glue the pinecone and green fabric leaf to the top of the lid.

Now, you have a bright and unique trick-or-treat can. Have a good time!

120

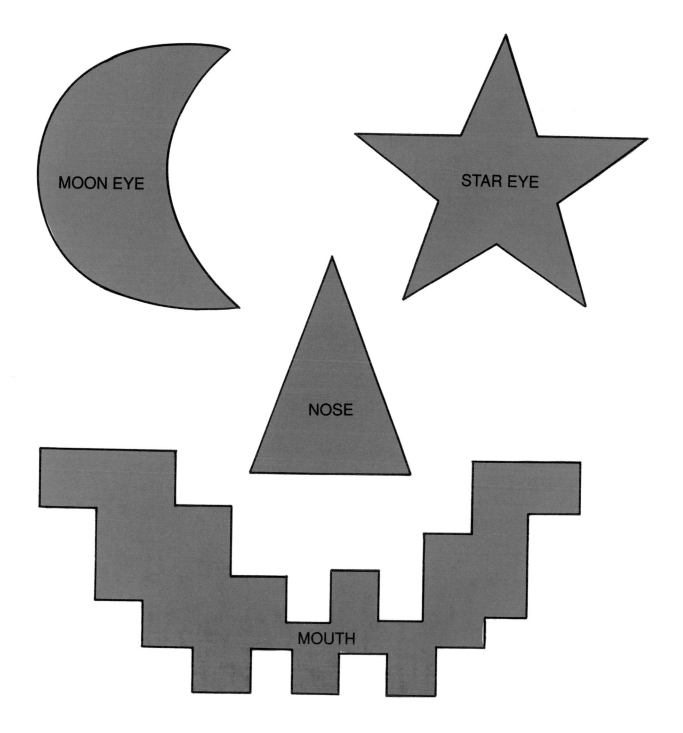

MOON EYE

STAR EYE

NOSE

MOUTH

Corny Witch Hands

Bewitched hands might bring a fright but not for long when you see they are made with popcorn and licorice. Eat up and then wear the ring yourself!

Ask a grown-up to help you purchase some of the check-list items.

CHECK LIST
(for 2 hands)

- ❏ Pair large clear plastic gloves
- ❏ Small pieces of licorice in 2 different colors
- ❏ 3 cups of popcorn, some white, some caramel or cheese
- ❏ 2 yards of ¼-inch-wide black gift ribbon
- ❏ 4 yards of ⅛-inch-wide orange curling gift ribbon
- ❏ Yardstick
- ❏ Scissors
- ❏ 2 small plastic spider rings

1 Put a piece of licorice in the finger tips of each glove. Use a different colored licorice for each hand.

2 Fill the gloves with popcorn. Use a different colored popcorn for each glove.

3 Cut the black ribbon into 2 pieces, each 36 inches long, and use the black ribbon to tie off the top of each glove.

4 Cut the orange ribbon into 4 pieces, each 36 inches long.

5 Tie 2 pieces of the orange ribbon around the top of each glove and use scissors to curl the ribbon. Put a plastic spider ring around 1 finger of each glove.

6 Put a plastic spider ring around 1 finger of each glove.

Liven up your Halloween party by giving spooky hands as party favors.

NOTE: You can make other witch hands. Buy more plastic gloves, ribbon, plastic rings, and different colored popcorn and licorice. Follow the directions and use your imagination.

Paper Twist Witch

A witch from a bottle can bring you good luck on Halloween night as a spooky centerpiece for the table.

Ask a grown-up to help you purchase some of the check-list items.

CHECK LIST

- ❑ ½ yard of 6-inch-wide green paper twist
- ❑ Ruler
- ❑ Scissors
- ❑ 6-inch craft foam ball
- ❑ Tacky glue
- ❑ Table knife
- ❑ 5-inch square of black felt
- ❑ Empty 20-ounce soda bottle
- ❑ 3 yards of 4-inch-wide black paper twist
- ❑ Pinking shears
- ❑ 6-inch-tall craft foam cone
- ❑ Tracing paper
- ❑ Pencil
- ❑ Construction paper: yellow, blue
- ❑ Straw raffia
- ❑ Pumpkin bell

MAKE HEAD

1 Before unwinding the green paper twist, use a ruler and scissors to cut 1 piece about 1½ inches long for the nose and 1 piece, about 13 inches long.

2 Untwist the 13-inch-long piece. Twist it in the middle and glue the twisted center to the top of the craft foam ball. The twisted center will become the center top of the head.

3 Wrap the paper twist around the ball, gluing the edges at the bottom.

4 Glue the green twist nose piece to the center front of the ball.

5 With a table knife, carefully cut a small hole in the bottom of the ball. Now, set the head aside.

MAKE BODY

1 Cut a 4-inch circle from the black felt. You might want to use a small bowl or round object as a guide for the circle.

2 Place the bottom of the soda bottle in the center of the felt circle and fold the sides of the circle up on the sides of the bottle. Glue the bottom and sides.

3 Before unwinding the black paper twist, cut 5 pieces for the witch's dress and cape, each about 8 inches long; 2 pieces for the sleeves, each 4 inches long; and 1 piece about 10 inches long.

4 Unwind 3 of the black dress pieces and glue the pieces vertically to the bottle to cover it completely. Look at the photograph.

5 Unwind the other 2 dress pieces of black paper twist and glue the top edges of each to the shoulder parts of the bottle to make a cape.

6 Before unwinding the green paper twist, cut 2 pieces for the arms, each about 5 inches long.

7 Glue a green paper twist arm to each side of the bottle. Fold the free ends back to make hands and glue.

8 Unwind the black sleeve pieces and wrap 1 piece around each arm. On each arm, glue at the long edge and then attach 1 short end to the body.

9 Unwind the 10-inch piece of black twist paper and cut it in half lengthwise so you have a strip 2-inches by 10-inches. Cut along 1 long edge with pinking shears.

10 Wrap and glue the edge of the strip around the bottle neck to make a collar.

MAKE HAT

1 Cut 2 pieces, each 8 inches long, from the black paper twist.

2 Unwind the paper and glue the pieces to cover the foam cone.

3 Cut a 16-inch piece from the black paper twist.

4 Unwind it and cut the piece in half lengthwise so you have a strip 2-inches by 16-inches.

5 Glue 1 long edge of the strip around the bottom of the cone until the short ends meet. The hat now has a brim.

6 Using tracing paper and a pencil, trace the moon and star patterns. Cut them out.

7 Place the patterns on the yellow construction paper. Trace and cut out 6 stars and 5 moons.

8 Place the patterns on the blue paper. Trace and cut out 3 stars and 2 moons.

9 Glue the moons and stars to the black hat and brim any way you would like.

STAR   MOON

ASSEMBLE PARTS

1 Put glue in the hole in the head and push the neck of the bottle into the hole.

2 Cut the straw raffia into 6-inch pieces.

3 Glue the raffia around the head to make the witch's hair.

4 Tie a bow in 1 bunch of the raffia and glue the bow under the collar.

5 Center and glue the hat on the top of the witch's head.

6 Glue the pumpkin bell to the point of the witch's hat.

Set the spooky witch out on the porch to welcome Halloween trick-or-treaters.

Shake-It-Up Witch

This witch mobile will bring smiles instead of screams to your next Halloween party. Have fun with such a wacky decoration.

Ask a grown-up to help you purchase some of the check-list items. Also ask a grown-up to help you use the oven to bake the clay.

CHECK LIST

- ❑ Sculpey clay: black (2 squares), white, red, green (1 square each)
- ❑ Rolling pin
- ❑ Tracing paper
- ❑ Pencil
- ❑ Scissors
- ❑ Table knife
- ❑ Toothpicks
- ❑ Access to an oven
- ❑ White glue
- ❑ Brush
- ❑ Aleene's Sand-Lastic colored sand: red, green, purple, yellow
- ❑ 1 yard thin orange paper cord

KNEAD & TRACE

1 Knead the clay in your hands until it is soft and easy to handle.

2 Use the rolling pin to roll the white clay into a 4-inch square, flat sheet.

3 Using tracing paper and a pencil, trace the hat, eyebrows, and mouth patterns on page 131. Cut them out.

4 Place the patterns on the black clay and cut them out using a table knife.

5 Roll the red clay into a long strip and mold it around the mouth to form lips.

6 Trace the nose, teeth, and moon patterns on page 131. Cut them out. Then, place them on the white clay and cut them out.

7 Add some crumbly white clay to the top of the nose to make it bumpy. Add 2 black clay dots for the nostrils and a green clay dot for a nose wart. Look at the photograph.

8 Stick the clay nose to the black eyebrows and stick the teeth into the mouth.

9 Roll 2 balls, each about ½", from the green clay and flatten them slightly to make the eyes.

10 Make two very small black clay dots for the pupils and stick them to the eyes. Look at the photograph.

POKE & BAKE

1 With a toothpick, poke 1 hole in the top of the hat, 2 holes in the bottom of the hat, 2 holes in the top of the eyebrows, 2 holes in the top lip of the mouth, and holes through each eye. Look at the patterns to see where to make the holes.

2 Ask a grown-up to help bake all the clay pieces according to the Sculpey directions. The white clay will turn a little darker during baking. Let the clay cool.

GLUE & DECORATE

1 Brush glue on the red of the mouth and sprinkle red sand over the glue.

2 Brush glue onto the black eyes (but not the pupils) and sprinkle the green sand on the eyes.

3 Brush glue on the black hat and sprinkle purple sand on the hat.

4 Brush glue on the moon and sprinkle yellow sand on it. Then, glue the moon to the hat. Look at the photograph to see how this should look.

THREAD & HANG

1 Cut the orange paper cord into 2 pieces, each 8 inches long, and into a 20-inch piece.

2 Tie a knot in an end of a short piece, leaving about ½-inch tail for the short end. Feed through the left hole in the hat and trim the short end close to the hole in the back of the hat.

3 Thread the long loose end through the left hole in the eyebrow from the front, leaving about ½ inch of cord between the hat and the eyebrow. Tie at the top of the eyebrow.

4 Now thread the loose end through an eye and tie a knot, leaving about ¼ inch of cord between the eyebrow and the eye.

5 Leaving about 1 inch between the eye and the mouth, thread the loose end through the left mouth hole and tie a knot. Then, trim the remaining loose end.

6 Repeat Steps 2, 3, 4, and 5 to thread the hat, eyebrow, eye, and mouth together on the right side.

7 Fold the 20-inch-long piece of orange cord in half and loop it through the top hole in the hat. Tie the loose ends into a knot. The witch now has a hanger.

You have a Super Sandy Witch Mobile. Bet your friends will want 1 of their own to liven up a Halloween party.

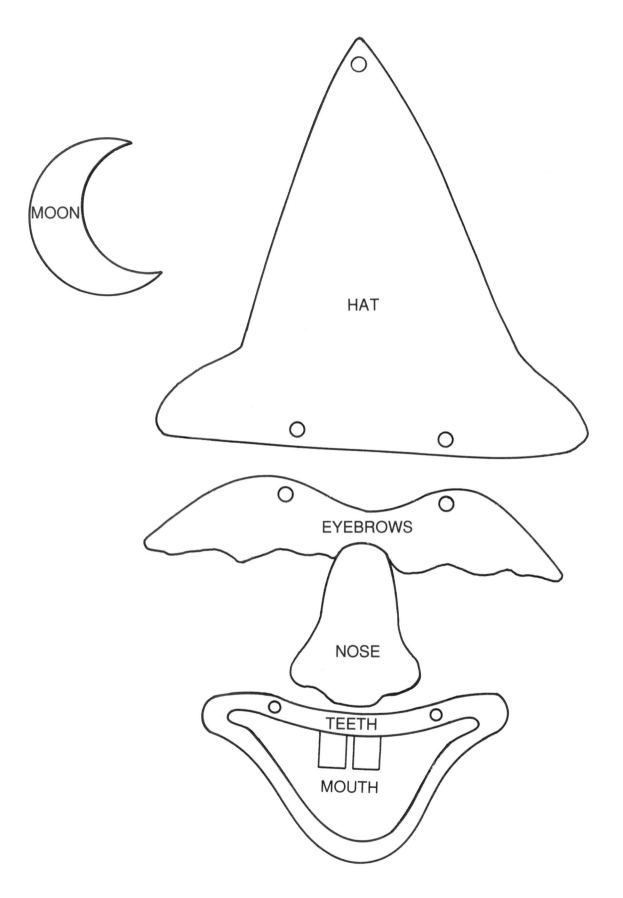

MOON

HAT

EYEBROWS

NOSE

TEETH

MOUTH

131

Ghastly Creepy Pals

Welcome Halloween spooks into your home. These are dark and creepy, but not too scary because you know where they come from and how they're made.

Ask a grown-up to help you purchase some of the check-list items. Also ask a grown-up to help you use the wire cutters.

GOOFY GHOST

CHECK LIST

❑ White or yellow gourd
❑ Tracing paper
❑ Pencil
❑ Carbon paper
❑ Clear tape
❑ Acrylic paints: white, black
❑ Paintbrush
❑ Spray resin

1 Select a gourd that has interesting twists and turns. Clean and dry the gourd.

2 Using tracing paper and a pencil, trace the eye pattern.

3 Tape a small piece of carbon paper to the gourd and tape the eye pattern over the carbon paper. Retrace the eye pattern. The carbon paper will transfer the eye pattern to the gourd.

4 Paint the eyes black and white. Look at the photograph to see how the eyes should look. Let the paint dry.

5 Spray the gourd with resin. Let the resin dry.

EYES

MIDNIGHT BAT

1 Cut a 24-inch piece of the black paper twist. Unravel the paper twist and place it flat on a work table.

2 Cut a jagged edge into both sides of the short ends of the paper twist. Look at the photograph to see how the ends of the wings should look.

3 Put a thin layer of glue in the middle 6 inches of the paper twist.

4 Place the foam craft ball in the middle and wrap the paper twist around the ball, making the edges meet. Overlap the edges and glue to secure.

5 As you wrap the paper over the ball, twist the paper at both sides of the ball. Glue at the twist close to the ball.

6 Fold out the paper twist ends to make the wings.

7 Use a ruler and chalk to draw 2 rectangles, each 3-inches by 1¼-inches, on the remaining black paper twist. Cut out the 2 rectangles.

8 Fold down the top 2 corners of the long side of the rectangle to make a triangle shape for the ear. Fold and make a crease about ¼ inch across the bottom of the ear. Do the same thing with the other rectangle.

9 Glue the bottom crease to the top of the bat's head so the ears stand up.

10 Glue the eyes under the ears.

SPOOKY SPIDER

CHECK LIST

- ❏ ½ yard of 12-inch-wide black paper twist
- ❏ Scissors
- ❏ Tacky glue
- ❏ 3-inch craft foam ball
- ❏ 5-inch craft foam ball
- ❏ Pair small glass eyes
- ❏ 1½ yards black paper-covered wire
- ❏ Wire cutters
- ❏ Ruler
- ❏ Chalk

1 Use a ruler and chalk to measure and mark a 6½-inch square and 10½-inch square on the black paper twist.

2 Cut out the 2 squares.

3 Twist the small square in the middle.

4 Put a thin layer of glue on the small foam ball and wrap the smaller piece of black paper around the ball completely. This is the spider's head.

5 Repeat Steps 3 and 4, using the large square and the large foam ball. This makes the spider's body.

6 Glue the head to the body.

7 Ask a grown-up to help you use the wire cutters to cut the wire into 2 pieces, each 1¼ inches long, and into 8 other pieces, each 5½ inches long.

8 Poke 4 of the longer wire pieces a little way into the body on 1 side, leaving about ½ inch between the pieces. Repeat with the other 4 wire pieces on the other side. Glue at the holes to secure. The spider now has 8 legs.

9 Poke the 2 shorter pieces of wire into the front center of the head about 1 inch apart. The spider now has a mouth.

10 Glue the eyes above the mouth.

It's nice to know you are adding a little ghoulishness to the year's scariest night.

Wacky Witch

*Here's a fun friend: a wacky witch who will add some color
and fright to any Halloween night!*

**Ask a grown-up to help you purchase
some of the check-list items. Also ask a
grown-up to help you use the paring knife
and iron.**

CHECK LIST

❑ 3-inch craft foam ball
❑ 4-inch craft foam ball
❑ Paring knife
❑ 3-inch canning jar ring
❑ Tracing paper
❑ Pencil
❑ Carbon paper
❑ Clear tape
❑ Scissors
❑ Iron-on double-sided transfer web
❑ Iron
❑ Tacky glue
❑ Acrylic paints: green, purple, black
❑ Wide paintbrush
❑ Narrow paintbrush
❑ Papier-mâché clay
❑ Ruler
❑ Straight pins
❑ Straw raffia
❑ ½ yard black fabric
❑ 10-inch-square purple fabric
❑ Scrap yellow fabric
❑ ¼ yard of ¼-inch-wide purple satin
   ribbon
❑ Papier-mâché pumpkin

CUT & TRACE

1 Ask a grown-up to help cut the craft foam balls with a paring knife. Decide what will be the bottom of the small ball. Cut off a small area to make it flat. Look at the diagram.

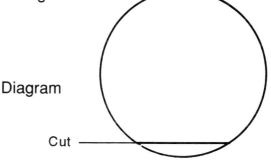

Diagram

Cut

2 Decide what will be the top of the large ball. Cut off a small area to make it flat. This will help the balls fit together better.

3 Using tracing paper and a pencil, trace the cape pattern on page 140. Cut the traced pattern out.

4 Position the tracing paper cape on the top center of the large foam ball and trace around it with a pencil.

PAINT & SCULPT

1 Paint the cape area black. Paint the bottom area purple. Look at the photograph to see how this should look. Let the paint dry. Set aside.

2 Paint the small craft foam ball green. Let the paint dry.

3 Shape a small amount of papier-mâché clay into a ½-inch-long cone shape for the nose.

4 Make a tiny ball of clay and stick it on the nose for a wart. Let the clay dry.

5 Paint the nose green and the wart black. Let the paint dry.

6 Paint the canning jar ring purple. Let the paint dry. Set aside.

7 Paint the papier-mâché pumpkin purple. Let the paint dry. Set aside.

FINISH FACE

1 Tape carbon paper to the green ball. Using tracing paper and a pencil, trace the face pattern.

2 Tape the traced face pattern to the green ball over the carbon paper; position the mouth about 1-inch above the flat part of the ball. Trace around the face again, and the carbon paper will transfer it to the ball.

3 Paint the eyes and the mouth black. Let the paint dry.

4 Look at the face pattern for nose placement. With a pencil, make a small hole in the green ball where the nose should go.

5 Put a drop of tacky glue in the hole. Insert the wide end of the clay nose into the hole. Let the glue dry. Set aside.

CUT & IRON

1 Cut a bunch of straw raffia into 5-inch pieces. Set aside.

2 Using tracing paper and a pencil, trace the large collar pattern on page 141 and cut it out. Pin it to the black fabric and cut out 1 collar.

3 From the remaining black fabric, cut 2 squares, measuring 15 inches each. Ask a grown-up to help you iron the transfer web between the fabric squares, fusing them together.

FACE

TRACE & CUT

1 Using tracing paper and a pencil, trace the hat and brim patterns on page 146 and cut them out. Pin them to the fused black square and cut 1 hat and 1 brim.

2 Trace the small collar pattern on page 141 and cut it out. Pin it to the purple fabric and cut out 1 collar.

3 Trace and cut out the moon and star patterns below. From the yellow fabric, cut out 5 stars and 4 moons. From the purple fabric, cut 3 stars and 2 moons.

ASSEMBLE & GLUE

1 Place the jar ring on the table with the flat edge down. Place the large ball on the jar ring. Make sure the flat side of the ball is at the top and that the purple side is on the bottom.

2 Glue the middle of the black collar to the center top of the ball. Glue the purple collar on top of the black collar. Glue the head on top of the purple collar with the flat side of the ball against the collar.

3 Glue 1 end of the raffia pieces to the middle top of the witch's head. Let the other end of the raffia pieces hang down around the head like hair on both the sides and the back.

4 Glue the fabric stars and moons to the brim and to the hat pieces.

5 Roll the hat piece into a cone. Overlap and glue where the fabric edges meet.

6 Glue the hat cone to the top of the head so it covers the top of the hair. Pull the brim down over the cone and glue along the base. Glue the purple ribbon around the hat to cover the brim seam.

7 With a pencil, punch a small hole in the bottom center of the pumpkin. Place a drop of glue in the hole. Put the tip of the hat in the hole to glue on the pumpkin.

MOON

STAR

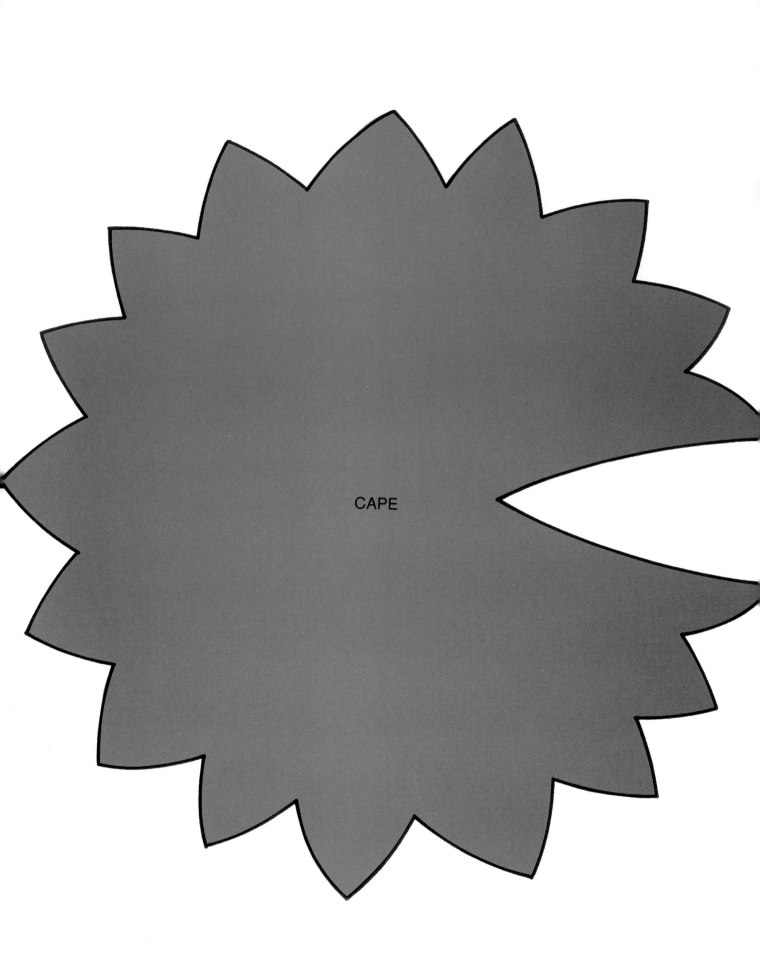

CAPE

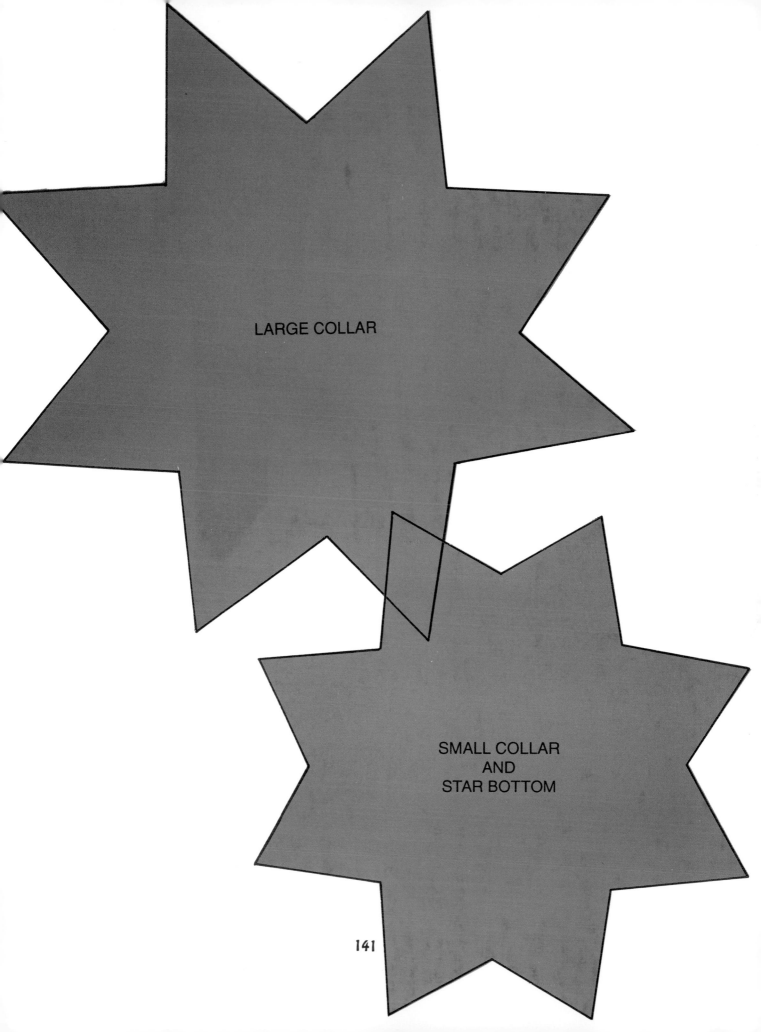

LARGE COLLAR

SMALL COLLAR
AND
STAR BOTTOM

Scruffy Scarecrow

Here's another fun friend: a scruffy scarecrow.
Put him to work entertaining you at play time.

CHECK LIST

- ❏ 3-inch craft foam ball
- ❏ 4-inch craft foam ball
- ❏ Paring knife
- ❏ 3-inch canning jar ring
- ❏ Tracing paper
- ❏ Pencil
- ❏ Carbon paper
- ❏ Clear tape
- ❏ Scissors
- ❏ Iron-on double-sided transfer web
- ❏ Iron
- ❏ Tacky glue
- ❏ Acrylic paints: orange, yellow, blue, black
- ❏ Wide paintbrushes
- ❏ Thin paintbrush
- ❏ ½-inch-round gold pierced earring
- ❏ 3 small green glass beads
- ❏ ½ yard brown fabric
- ❏ 10-inch square of blue/white checked fabric
- ❏ 10-inch square of blue dotted white fabric
- ❏ Straw raffia
- ❏ Scrap red gingham fabric
- ❏ Scrap white dotted purple fabric
- ❏ Pinking shears

CUT & TRACE

1 Ask a grown-up to help cut the craft foam balls with a paring knife. Decide what will be the bottom of the small ball. Cut off a small area to make it flat. Look at the diagram on page 137.

2 Decide what will be the top of the large ball. Cut off a small area to make it flat. This will help the balls fit together better.

3 Using tracing paper and a pencil, trace the star bottom pattern on page 141. Cut the traced pattern out.

4 Position the tracing paper star bottom on the bottom of the large ball. Trace around it with a pencil.

PAINT & GLUE

1 Paint the star bottom blue. Paint the top area yellow. Look at the photograph. Let the paint dry.

2 With a thin brush, paint a vertical black line down the front of the large ball just over the yellow area.

3 On 1 side of the line, paint a ½-inch by ¼-inch rectangle for the pocket. Repeat on the other side. Look at the photograph.

4 Put glue on 1 side of a green glass bead. Press the bead into the foam ball on the right side of the black line to make a button. Repeat with the 2 remaining beads to make a row of buttons.

5 Take the back clasp off the pierced earing. Push the post into the foam ball in the center of the right pocket to resemble a pocket watch. Set the ball aside.

PAINT & TRACE

1 Paint the small ball orange. Let the paint dry.

2 Tape carbon paper to the orange ball with the carbon side down. Using tracing paper and a pencil, trace the face pattern.

3 Tape the traced face pattern to the orange ball over the carbon paper; position the mouth about ½ inch above the flat part of the orange ball. Trace over the face pattern again, the carbon paper will transfer it to the ball.

4 Paint the eyes, nose and mouth black. Let the paint dry.

5 Paint the canning jar ring blue. Let the paint dry.

CUT & IRON

1 Cut a bunch of straw raffia into 5-inch pieces. Cut a smaller bunch into 3-inch pieces. Set aside.

2 Using tracing paper and a pencil, trace the large collar pattern on page 141. Cut it out. Pin it to the blue/white checked fabric and cut out 1 collar. Set aside.

3 From the brown fabric, cut 2 squares measuring 15 inches each. Ask a grown-up to help you iron the transfer web between the squares, fusing them together.

4 Using tracing paper and a pencil, trace the hat and brim patterns on page 146 and cut them out. Pin them to the fused brown square and cut out 1 hat and 1 brim.

5 Trace the small collar pattern on page 141 and cut it out. Pin it to the blue-dotted white fabric and cut 1 collar.

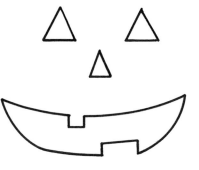

FACE

6 With the pinking shears, cut a 1¼-inch by 1½-inch rectangle from the red gingham fabric scrap.

7 Also with shears, cut a 1¼-inch by 1½-inch rectangle and a 1-inch square from the white-dotted purple fabric.

8 Glue the small purple square to the hat brim. Glue the large purple rectangle and the red square to the hat piece. Let the glue dry.

9 Roll the hat into a cone. Overlap and glue where the fabric edges meet.

10 Cut off the tip of the hat with pinking shears. Insert 3-inch pieces of straw raffia. Glue to secure.

ASSEMBLE & GLUE

1 Place the canning jar ring on the table with the flat edge down. Place the large foam ball on the jar ring. Make sure the flat side of the ball is at the top and the blue side is on the bottom.

2 Glue the middle of the blue/white checked collar to the center top of the ball. Glue the blue dotted white collar on top of the checked collar.

3 Glue the head on top of the dotted collar with the flat side of the ball against the collar.

4 Glue 1 end of the straw raffia pieces to the middle top of the head. Let the other end of the pieces hang around the head like hair.

5 Glue the hat to the top of the head so it covers the top of the raffia hair. Pull the brim down over the cone and glue along the base.

6 Fold down the top half of the hat. Ask a grown-up to help iron a crease at the fold to make the hat flop over.

These friends will be around a long time to bring some fun to any Autumn day.

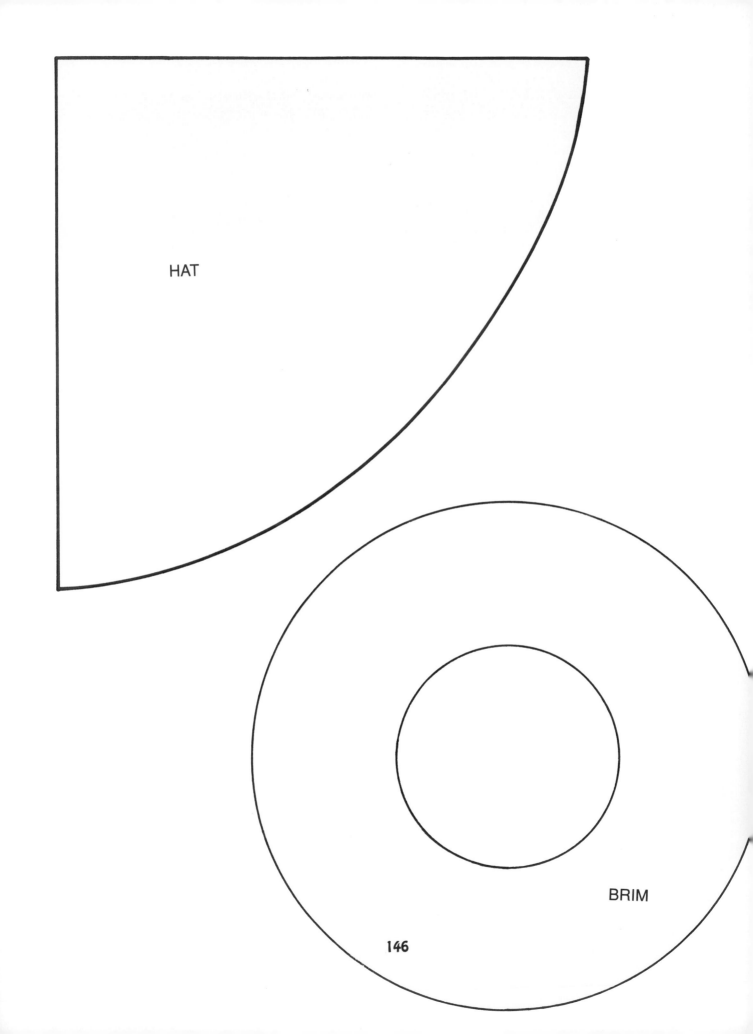

HAT

BRIM

Lucky Turkey Apron

Make a special apron for a special day – Thanksgiving Day.
Wear the apron to greet guests or help cook in the kitchen.
Look at the photograph on page 148.

Ask a grown-up to help you purchase some of the check-list items.

CHECK LIST

❑ White apron that fits you
❑ Tracing paper
❑ Pencil
❑ Masking tape
❑ Fabric paints: brown, peach, pink, yellow
❑ Black medium-tip permanent marker

TRACE & TRANSFER

1 Using tracing paper and a pencil, trace the turkey pattern and the words "Happy Thanksgiving" on page 149.

2 Tape the traced patterns to a window through which daylight is coming.

3 Tape the apron over the pattern. You will see the pattern through the apron.

4 Using a pencil, trace the patterns onto the apron.

PAINT & OUTLINE

1 Paint the turkey on the apron any way you would like. Look at the photograph for an idea of how it should look.

2 Paint the hearts in the "Happy Thanksgiving" message pink.

3 Use the black marker to outline the turkey and to outline the message. Also use it to draw an eye on the turkey.

● ● ● ● ● ● ● ● ● ● ● ● ● ● ●

Now that you've got the uniform, get to work! There's a lot of food to cook.

● ● ● ● ● ● ● ● ● ● ● ● ● ● ●

Happy Thanksgiving!

Gingerbread Boy Stocking

Stockings are a traditional part of Christmas festivities.
This gingerbread boy stocking is big enough to hold a bunch of treats.

CHECK LIST
(for 1 stocking)

- ❏ 2 wood gingerbread boy cutouts, 4 inches tall
- ❏ 2 wood gingerbread boy cutouts, 2 inches tall
- ❏ Acrylic paints: tan, red, forest green
- ❏ Paintbrushes
- ❏ Ruler
- ❏ Pencil
- ❏ Straight pins
- ❏ 1 yard 45-inch-wide canvas
- ❏ Straight pins
- ❏ Scissors
- ❏ 1-inch wood cube
- ❏ Ruler
- ❏ 2 yards of ¾-inch-wide red satin ribbon
- ❏ 2 yards of ⅛-inch-wide green satin ribbon
- ❏ 2 yards of 1⁄16-inch-wide red satin ribbon
- ❏ ¾ yard of ¼-inch-wide green satin ribbon
- ❏ Sewing machine
- ❏ Brown thread
- ❏ Wood beads: red, brown, green (2 each color)
- ❏ ½-inch buttons: 1 green, 2 white, 2 blue
- ❏ Tacky glue

PAINT & TRACE

1 Paint all the gingerbread cutouts tan. Let the paint dry.

2 Paint red stripes on the hands and feet. Look at the photograph to see where to paint the stripes. Let the paint dry.

3 Using a ruler and a pencil, draw a 9-inch-long horizontal line about 1 inch from the top edge of the canvas.

4 From each end of that line, draw a stocking about 18 inches long. Look at the diagram on page 153 to see how to shape the stocking.

5 Cut out the stocking piece. Pin it to the remaining canvas and trace around it. Cut out the second stocking piece.

6 On 1 stocking piece, paint the cuff, toe, and heel forest green. Paint red outlines at the cuff, heel, and toe. Look at the photograph. Let the paint dry.

7 Paint the rest of the stocking piece tan. Turn the second stocking piece so the toe faces the opposite direction, and paint it tan. This will be the back of the stocking.

8 Dip 1 side of the wood cube into the red paint. Stamp the cube, with a point at the top, onto the green cuff of the first stocking piece. Continue stamping to make a row of red diamonds across the green cuff. Look at the photograph to see how this should look.

CUT & SEW

1 Use a ruler and scissors to cut the wide red satin ribbon into 2 pieces, each 34-inches long, and 1 piece, about 4 inches long.

2 Again, use the ruler and scissors to cut the narrow green satin ribbon into 2 pieces, each 36-inches long.

3 Cut the narrow red ribbon in 2 pieces, each 36-inches long.

4 Cut 1 piece of the wide green ribbon, about 27-inches long.

5 Ask a grown-up to help you sew the 2 stocking pieces together. With the wrong sides facing, use brown thread to topstitch the pieces together ¼ inch from the edges. Leave the top open.

6 Fold the 4-inch piece of red ribbon in half. Place the free edges of the ribbon between the edges of the top right corner of the stocking. Ask a grown-up to topstitch the ribbon hanger into place with a ¼-inch seam.

GLUE & TIE

1 Glue the green button in the middle of the center red diamond on the green cuff of the stocking

2 Glue a white button in the center of a diamond on each side of the green button, and glue a blue button on the diamonds on the other side of the white buttons.

3 Tie the 2 large and 2 small gingerbread boy cutouts and 2 green, 2 brown, and 2 red beads to the ends of the 2 pieces of narrow green ribbon and to the 2 pieces of the narrow red ribbon. Look at the photograph.

4 Tie 1 piece of the wide red ribbon into a double bow.

5 Grasp the red double bow and the ends of the narrow red and green ribbons (with the cutouts) together at the center.

6 Pull the wide green ribbon through the hanger on the stocking and around the ribbons in your hand and tie a knot to attach the ribbons to the stocking.

7 Tie the other piece of wide red ribbon into a bow around all the ribbons.

Now you have a gingerbread boy stocking to hang on Christmas Eve.

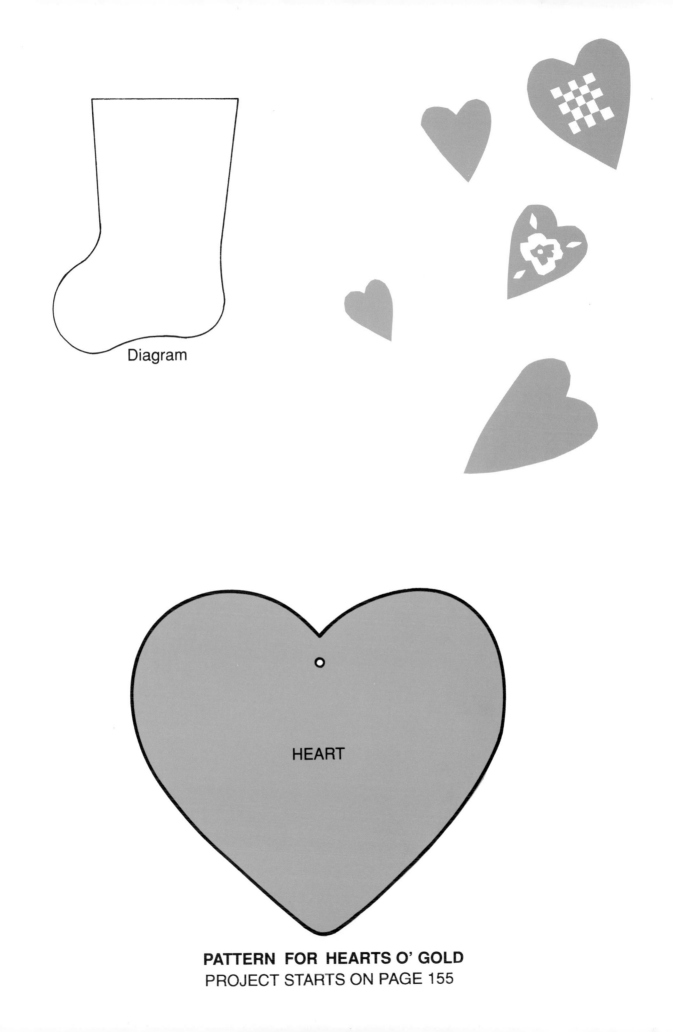

Diagram

HEART

PATTERN FOR HEARTS O' GOLD
PROJECT STARTS ON PAGE 155

Hearts O' Gold

You can decorate the entire Christmas tree with these glittering hearts or just make 1 to give as a gift.

Ask a grown-up to help you purchase some of the check-list items.

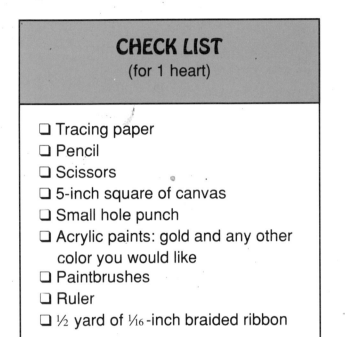

CHECK LIST
(for 1 heart)

❑ Tracing paper
❑ Pencil
❑ Scissors
❑ 5-inch square of canvas
❑ Small hole punch
❑ Acrylic paints: gold and any other color you would like
❑ Paintbrushes
❑ Ruler
❑ ½ yard of 1/16-inch braided ribbon

TRACE & PAINT

1 Using tracing paper and a pencil, trace the heart pattern on page 153. Cut it out.

2 Place the pattern on the canvas and cut out 1 heart.

3 Punch a small hole in the top center of the heart.

4 Paint the heart on both sides any color you would like. Let the paint dry.

5 Add gold paint accents. Look at the photograph to see how to paint the heart.

CUT & HANG

1 Cut the braided ribbon into 2 pieces, each 9 inches long.

2 To make the hanger, thread 1 ribbon piece through the hole in the heart and tie a knot close to the heart. Then, knot the long ends of the ribbon.

3 Thread the other ribbon piece through the same hole and tie into a bow.

Let your Hearts O' Gold bring some light and warmth to the holidays.

NOTE: These Hearts O' Gold are so easy to make that you probably will want to make several. If you purchase 1/8 yard of canvas, 5 yards of the ribbon, and acrylic paints in several colors, you will have enough material to make 10 hearts. Follow the same directions, using different colors.

Snow Puff Ornament

*The holidays are more festive when you make decorations yourself.
Display this snowman on the tree or in a window.*

Ask a grown-up to help you purchase some of the check-list items. Also ask a grown-up to help you use the sewing machine and hot glue gun.

CHECK LIST

- ❏ 10-inch by 18-inch piece of white fabric
- ❏ White thread
- ❏ Sewing machine
- ❏ Polyester stuffing
- ❏ 1-inch by 10-inch torn strip of blue fabric
- ❏ 5 medium black beads
- ❏ 7 tiny black beads
- ❏ Small wood or plastic carrot
- ❏ Black felt hat
- ❏ Black crochet thread
- ❏ Needle
- ❏ Hot glue gun and glue sticks

1 Fold the white fabric so the long edges meet and the right sides are facing. Ask a grown-up to help you sew a ¼-inch seam down the long edge. This will give you a fabric tube.

2 Tie a knot at 1 end of the tube and turn it inside out. The knot will become the bottom of the tube.

3 Take a handful of the stuffing and stuff it into the bottom of the tube. Shape it into a ball, about 5 inches wide. Use white thread to tie the top of the ball off.

4 Take more stuffing and make a 4-inch-wide ball for the middle. Tie with thread. Make a 3-inch-wide ball for the head and tie the top off with thread.

5 Glue 3 of the medium-sized beads in a row down the front of the middle ball for buttons. Glue the other 2 medium-sized black beads to the top ball for the eyes.

6 Glue the carrot piece under the eyes to make a nose. Glue the 7 small beads in a curved line to make the mouth.

7 Tie the strip of blue fabric around the neck for a scarf.

8 Thread an 8-inch piece of the crochet thread through the top of the felt hat and tie the ends into a knot. Glue the hat to the snowman's head.

Hang your soft snowman with pride to welcome holiday guests.

Soft Flight Angel

*This angel mobile, which shows off your painting skills,
looks great in a nursery or even in your room.*

**Ask a grown-up to help you purchase
some of the check-list items.**

CHECK LIST

- ❑ Watercolor paper
- ❑ Watercolor paints: blue, green,
  purple, pink, red
- ❑ Paintbrushes
- ❑ Tracing paper
- ❑ Pencil
- ❑ Scissors
- ❑ Tacky glue
- ❑ Colored pencils: brown, red, pink
- ❑ Needle
- ❑ Pink embroidery floss
- ❑ Masking tape

COLOR & TRACE

1 Paint 1 side of the watercolor paper in blues and purples. Let the colors blend. Let the paint dry.

2 Paint the other side of the watercolor paper in shades of pink. Let the paint dry.

3 Using tracing paper and a pencil, trace the angel, bird, and butterfly patterns on page 160. Cut out the patterns.

4 Position the patterns on the watercolor paper and trace around them. Cut out 1 angel, 2 birds, and 3 butterflies.

5 Cut out 1 extra head from the paper. Glue that head to the purple side of the angel so the pink side of the head shows. The angel now has a pink head on its purple side and on its pink side.

6 Draw the face pattern onto both sides of the angel head.

7 Use a pink pencil to color the cheeks and the nose. Outline the nose and color the eyes and hair with a dark brown pencil. Outline the mouth in red.

159

KNOT & THREAD

1 Use the needle to poke tiny holes in the head and wings of the angel and into the birds and butterflies. Look at the patterns to see where to make the holes.

2 Tie a knot in 1 end of the embroidery floss. Thread the other end of the floss through the hole in the pink side of a butterfly and tie a knot.

3 Leave about ¼ inch of the floss and then, tie another knot.

4 Thread the loose end of the floss through the second butterfly. Tie a knot.

5 Repeat Steps 3 and 4 to string the third butterfly.

6 Take the loose end of the floss and thread it through the middle hole in the angel and tie a knot and cut the floss. The 3 butterflies now hang down from the bottom center of the angel.

7 Take another piece of floss, tie a knot, and thread the loose end through the hole in 1 of the birds. Tie a knot and then, thread the floss through the hole in the left angel's wing. Tie a knot and cut the floss.

8 Repeat Step 7, using the second bird and attaching it to the angel's right wing.

9 Thread another piece of floss through the hole in the angel's head. Make a loop and tie the 2 ends together for a hanger.

■ ● ★ ■ ● ★ ■ ● ★ ■ ● ★ ■

Hang your angel in front of a slightly open window and watch her flutter.

■ ● ★ ■ ● ★ ■ ● ★ ■ ● ★ ■

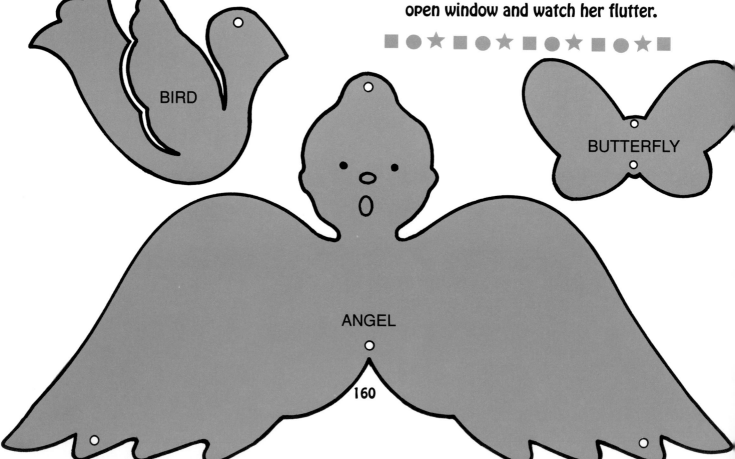

BIRD

BUTTERFLY

ANGEL

160

Chewy Choo-Choo

Make a choo-choo train that's a toy and a snack.
The simple directions will give you a nifty gift for a friend or for yourself.
Look at the photograph on page 162.

Ask a grown-up to help you purchase some of the check-list items.

CHECK LIST

- ❏ 8 green paper clips
- ❏ 5 packs chewing gum (5 sticks per pack)
- ❏ Tacky glue
- ❏ 20 individually wrapped round candy mints
- ❏ Large roll of assorted candy circles
- ❏ Individually wrapped cinnamon candy drop
- ❏ Chocolate candy kiss
- ❏ 4 individually wrapped chewy candy squares
- ❏ 3 small rolls candy tarts
- ❏ 5 candy root beer barrels

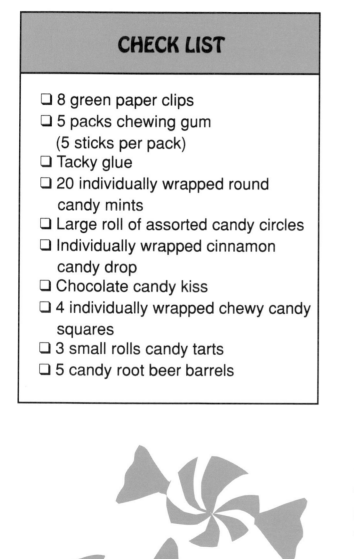

MAKE ENGINE & CABOOSE

1 Unfold and bend the 8 paper clips so each makes an S shape.

2 Glue 1 paper clip to the bottom wide side of a pack of gum so half of the paper clip S extends beyond the end of the pack. Look at Diagram A to see how this should look.

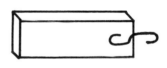

Diagram A

3 Repeat Step 2 with another pack of gum and a paper clip.

4 Position 1 of these packs of gum so the paper clip is on the bottom and to the back. Glue the large roll of circle candy to the top of the pack of gum.

5 Glue the cinnamon candy to the front of the pack and the roll of circle candy.

6 Glue the candy kiss to the front top of the roll of candy, and glue a chewy candy square to the back of the candy roll and gum pack.

7 Position the other pack of gum so the paper clip is on the bottom and to the front. Glue a chewy candy square to the middle top of the gum pack.

8 Glue 2 candy mints to each side of the 2 packs of gum to make wheels. Look at the photograph to see how the engine and caboose should look.

MAKE CARS

1 Glue 2 paper clips, 1 on each end, to the 3 remaining packs of gum. Look at Diagram B.

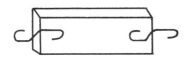

Diagram B

2 Glue 2 candy mints to each side of each pack of gum to make wheels for these cars.

3 For the first car, glue 3 small candy tart rolls stacked on top of the gum pack.

4 For the second car, glue 2 chewy squares to the top of the gum pack.

5 For the third car, glue the 5 root beer barrels stacked on top of the gum pack. (Since they are not wrapped, you will not be able to eat the barrels.)

6 Hook the gum packs together using the paper clips to make the train.

This sweet train can take you to a party where you can tear it apart and share.

Sugar-Charged Airplanes

A fast treat, the airplanes won't take long to create or to devour.
Share the sweetness with family or friends.

Ask a grown-up to help you purchase some of the check-list items.

CHECK LIST
(for 3 airplanes)

- ❑ 3 large rolls of candy circles
- ❑ Piece of individually wrapped taffy
- ❑ 6 individually wrapped sticks of gum
- ❑ 2 individually wrapped chewy candy rolls
- ❑ Small roll of candy circles
- ❑ Individually wrapped candy mint
- ❑ Individually wrapped chocolate heart
- ❑ Tacky glue

FIRST PLANE

1 Glue a piece of taffy to 1 end of 1 of the large rolls of candy circles. This makes the plane's propeller.

2 Glue 1 stick of gum horizontally across the top and 1 across the bottom of the candy roll just behind the taffy. The plane now has wings.

3 Glue a small chewy candy roll under the bottom gum stick. Look at the photograph to see how this should look.

SECOND PLANE

1 Repeat Steps 1, 2, and 3 above, using the candy mint for the propeller.

THIRD PLANE

1 Repeat Steps 1, 2, and 3 again, this time using the chocolate heart for the propeller and gluing the small roll of candy circles under the stick of gum.

You are ready to take off with your hand-built airplanes that are fueled with sugar.

Peachy Flower Basket

Do baskets in the store cost more than what's in your piggy bank? Make this one.
It's quick, dainty, and has one plus not found in the store—you create it.

Ask a grown-up to help you purchase some of the check-list items.

CHECK LIST

- ☐ Large balloon
- ☐ Fabric stiffener
- ☐ Pie tin
- ☐ Spool of peach crochet thread
- ☐ Pencil
- ☐ Scissors
- ☐ 1 yard of 1½-inch-wide ivory gathered lace
- ☐ 2 yards of 1-inch-wide gold-trimmed ivory wired ribbon
- ☐ Small dried red and pink roses
- ☐ Small cloth leaves

WRAP & DRY

1 Inflate the balloon.

2 Pour the fabric stiffener into a pie tin.

3 Pull the peach thread through the fabric stiffener.

4 Wrap the thread around the balloon, overlapping the thread until the balloon is almost completely covered, leaving only small openings. Let the thread dry.

5 After the thread is completely dry, pop the balloon and pull it out through the thread. If the balloon sticks, pull slowly so you don't damage the basket shape.

167

OUTLINE & CUT

1 To mark the handle, use a pencil and outline 2 half circles on the top half of the ball. Make the curved edges of the 2 half circles about 2 inches apart. Look at the diagram to see how to do this.

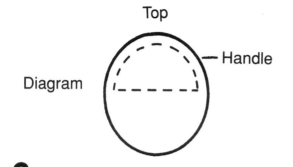

Top

Diagram — Handle

2 Cut out the half circles, opening the top of the basket but leaving the 2-inch-wide handle intact.

3 Pull more thread through the fabric stiffener in the pie tin.

4 Lay the thread across and around the raw edges. Let the thread dry. This will reinforce the basket edges and handle.

CUT & GLUE

1 Cut a 25-inch piece of ivory lace.

2 Glue the lace piece around the basket rim, matching the short ends and trimming the excess.

3 Cut the gold-trimmed ivory ribbon into 2 pieces, each 30-inches long.

4 Gather 1 piece with your fingers and glue it around the basket rim along the top edge of the lace. Look at the photograph to see how this should look.

5 Tie the second piece of gold-trimmed ribbon into a bow with 10-inch-long tails.

6 Cut a V in each tail end.

7 Glue the bow to the top middle of the basket handle.

8 Twist and gather the tail lengths along the handle and glue. Look at the photograph to see how this should look.

9 Glue the dried roses and cloth leaves to the handle as you would like. Again, look at the photograph.

String Evergreen

Make a delicate centerpiece from string and dried flowers.
Look at the photograph on page 166.

Ask a grown-up to help you purchase some of the check-list items.

CHECK LIST

- ❏ 9½-inch-tall craft foam cone
- ❏ Plastic wrap
- ❏ Masking tape
- ❏ Fabric stiffener
- ❏ Pie tin
- ❏ Spool sage green crochet thread
- ❏ Dried red rosebuds
- ❏ Dried small pink flowers
- ❏ ¼ yard of ¼-inch-wide sage green satin ribbon
- ❏ Tacky glue

WRAP & DRY

1 Wrap a layer of plastic around the cone. Secure with masking tape.

2 Pour the fabric stiffener into a pie tin.

3 Pull the green crochet thread through the fabric stiffener.

4 Wrap the thread around the plastic-covered cone. Overlap the thread until the cone is almost completely covered, leaving only small openings. Let the thread dry.

PULL & GLUE

1 After the thread is completely dry, take it off the cone. If it sticks to the plastic, pull slowly so you do not damage the tree shape of the thread.

2 Glue the rosebuds and flowers to the bottom and sides of the tree. Look at the photograph to see how this should look.

3 Twist the ribbon along the side near the roses and glue at intervals to secure.

The basket and tree make unique centerpieces to brighten your holiday table.

Cushy Christmas Tree

Can you glue and paint? Then, you can put this bright holiday pillow together in just a few minutes. The look is simple but classy for Christmas Day.

Ask a grown-up to help you purchase some of the items.

CHECK LIST

- ❑ 11-inch by 13-inch purchased red throw pillow
- ❑ 1 yard of ¼-inch-wide green double-fold bias tape
- ❑ Tacky glue
- ❑ Tracing paper
- ❑ Pencil
- ❑ Scissors
- ❑ Fabric chalk
- ❑ Acrylic paints: yellow, brown
- ❑ Paintbrush

1 Glue 1 end of the green bias tape to the pillow centered about 2 inches down from the top edge.

2 Slant the tape at a angle downward and to the right for about 2 inches and then, glue the tape into place on the pillow. Look at the photograph.

3 Fold the bias tape back at an angle to make a point and glue to pillow front.

4 Extend the tape at an angle downward and to the left for about 3 inches. Make point and glue.

5 Repeat the same steps, making a zigzag with the tape. Be sure to make each step in the zigzag about 1 or 2 inches longer than the step above so the tree gets wider. Look at the photograph to see how to position tape.

6 Stop attaching the tape to the pillow about 2 inches from the bottom edge.

7 Using tracing paper and a pencil, trace the star pattern. Cut it out.

8 Place the pattern just above the top of your tape tree and use fabric chalk to trace the outline onto the pillow.

9 Trace and cut out the trunk pattern and place it below the last strip of tape. Center and trace around it with chalk.

10 Paint the star yellow and the trunk brown. Let the paint dry.

Simple! But make it too quickly and someone will want you to make another!

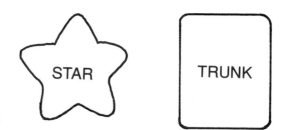

171

Wood-Block Frosty

Here's a snowman who won't melt when the sun comes out. Have fun building this frosty guy out of wood blocks instead of winter's cold snow.

Ask a grown-up to help you purchase some of the check-list items.

CHECK LIST

- ❏ Wood cube, 1¼ inch
- ❏ 5 wood blocks:
    2-inches by 1¼-inches by ½-inch
    2¾-inches by 1½-inches by ½-inch
    3-inches by 1½-inches by 2-inches
    4-inches by 1½-inches by 4-inches
    5-inches by 1½-inches by 5-inches
- ❏ Acrylic paints: white, blue, black
- ❏ Paintbrushes
- ❏ Tracing paper
- ❏ Pencil
- ❏ Carbon paper
- ❏ Black permanent marker
- ❏ Fine-grade sandpaper
- ❏ 7 medium-size round black beads
- ❏ 3 large round black beads
- ❏ Orange plastic carrot, ¼ inch long
- ❏ 6 thin twigs, each about ¼ inch long
- ❏ Tacky glue

PAINT & TRACE

1 Paint the cube and all the blocks white. Let the paint dry.

2 Dry-brush paint the cube and the 2 smallest blocks with blue paint. Without dipping the brush in any water, brush the blue on lightly. Do not cover the surface fully. Let some of the white paint show through. Let the paint dry.

3 To make the black top hat, place the cube and the 2 small blocks flat on your work table. Paint the front edge of each black. See the diagram. Let the paint dry.

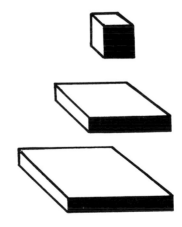

Diagram

4 Using tracing paper and a pencil, trace the snowman's head, middle, and bottom patterns.

5 Tape the carbon paper to the remaining 3 wood blocks with the carbon side against the wood. Tape the traced patterns over the carbon paper and trace around the patterns again. See the photograph to see how to place the patterns on the blocks.

6 Dry-brush paint the 3 large blocks blue, leaving the head, middle, and bottom of the snowman and about ¼ inch across the bottom of the largest block completely white. Let the blue paint dry.

OUTLINE & GLUE

1 Use black marker to outline around the snowman's head, middle, and bottom.

2 Use sandpaper to sand along the outside edges and surfaces of the blocks to let some of the white paint show through the blue.

3 Glue the twigs onto the middle block to make the snowman's hands. Look at the photograph to see how to place the twigs.

4 Remove the green leaves, if any, from the plastic carrot. Glue the carrot to the snowman's head to make a nose.

5 Glue the medium black beads to the face to make the eyes and a mouth.

6 Glue the large black beads to the middle to make buttons. Look at the photograph and patterns to see where to place the beads.

7 Stack the blocks on top of one another from the largest at the bottom to the smallest at the top to finish your wood block snowman.

Have fun with the blocks that make up your snowman's funny head and body.

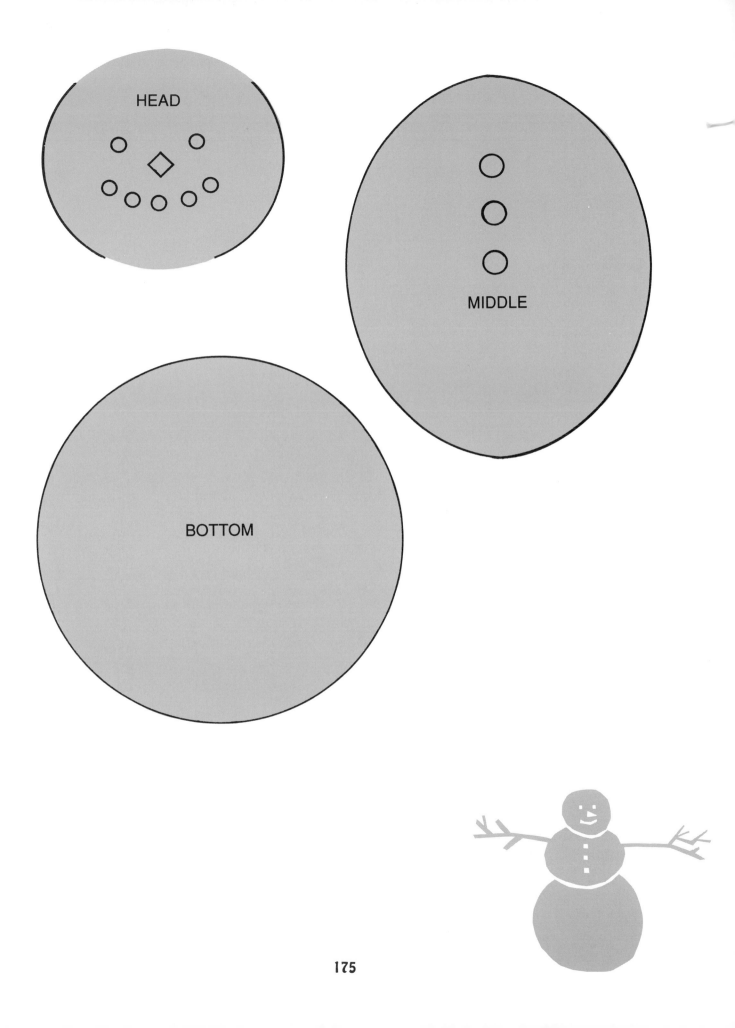

HEAD

MIDDLE

BOTTOM

Ripped St. Nicks

Can Christmas decorating really be this simple? Of course, it can. Tear fabric and glue on holiday trinkets to make festive Santa Claus ornaments.

Ask a grown-up to help you purchase some of the check-list items.

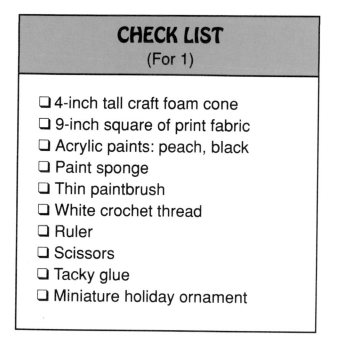

CHECK LIST
(For 1)

- ❑ 4-inch tall craft foam cone
- ❑ 9-inch square of print fabric
- ❑ Acrylic paints: peach, black
- ❑ Paint sponge
- ❑ Thin paintbrush
- ❑ White crochet thread
- ❑ Ruler
- ❑ Scissors
- ❑ Tacky glue
- ❑ Miniature holiday ornament

TEAR & PAINT

1 Tear the print fabric into 1¼-inch strips. Set aside 1 strip.

2 Glue the strips to the cone, over-lapping and covering the cone completely.

3 With a sponge and peach paint, paint a face in an oval shape, starting the top of the face about ½ inch below the point of the cone. Let the paint dry.

4 With the handle end of a paintbrush, paint the eyes black. Let the paint dry.

CUT & KNOT

1 For the beard, cut the crochet thread into 50 or more 1-inch-long pieces.

2 Glue pieces about ⅛ inch below the eyes on the face.

3 For the arms, wrap the 9-inch by 1¼-inch strip that you had set aside around the cone with the ends coming together in the front of the cone.

4 Loop 1 end through the ornament. Tie the ends together into a tight knot. Glue the strip to the body to secure.

Make as many St. Nicks in as many colors as you'd like. Hang them on the tree or in a window to add to the holiday excitement.

Hang-Around Santa

Make and display a mobile as a new twist to Christmas decorating. The Santa is just cute enough to decorate your room all year long.

Ask a grown-up to help you purchase some of the check-list items. Also ask a grown-up to help you use the oven to bake the clay.

CHECK LIST

- ❑ Sculpey clay: white, red, black (1 square each)
- ❑ Rolling pin
- ❑ Tracing paper
- ❑ Pencil
- ❑ Scissors
- ❑ Table knife
- ❑ Ruler
- ❑ Toothpicks
- ❑ Access to an oven
- ❑ White glue
- ❑ Brush
- ❑ Aleene's Sand-Lastic colored sand: red, green
- ❑ 1 yard thin green paper cord

KNEAD & TRACE

1 Knead the clay in your hands until it is soft and easy to handle. (If the clay becomes too stretchy, put it in the refrigerator for a short time.)

2 Use the rolling pin to roll the white clay into a 4-inch square flat sheet. Do the same with the red clay.

3 Using tracing paper and a pencil, trace the beard and the 2 fur patterns on page 181. Cut out the patterns.

4 Place the patterns on the white clay and cut around them with the table knife.

5 Trace the hat pattern on page 181 and cut it out. Place the hat pattern on the red clay and cut it out with the table knife.

6 Crumble the remaining white clay and press onto the fur pieces and the beard.

POKE & BAKE

1 Roll a small (about ¼ inch) red clay ball for the nose, 2 medium-sized black balls for the eyes and 2 small black balls for the pupils of the eyes. Stick the pupils to the front middle of the eyes.

2 Place the white fur pieces on the red hat and push together to secure. Look at the photograph to see how to place fur.

3 With the toothpicks, poke 1 hole in the top of the hat, 1 hole through each black ball, 1 through the beard, and 3 through the hat fur. Look at the patterns to see where to make the holes.

4 Ask a grown-up to help bake all the clay pieces according to the Sculpey directions. The white clay will turn a little darker during baking. Let the clay cool completely.

GLUE & ASSEMBLE

1 Brush the glue onto the red part of the hat and sprinkle red sand over the glue. Do the same with the red nose.

2 Brush the glue on the black eyes (not on the pupils) and sprinkle green sand on the eyes, leaving the pupils black.

3 Cut the green paper cord into 2 pieces, each about 1½-inches long, into a 2½-inch piece and into a 20-inch piece.

4 Tie a knot in an end of a short piece of cord, leaving a ½-inch tail for the short end. Feed through the hole in the black/green eye. Look at the diagram.

5 Trim the short end close to the hole in the eye. Tie the loose end to the left hole in the hat fur in the same way.

Diagram

6 Repeat Steps 4 and 5 with the other eye, attaching it to the right hole in the fur on the hat.

7 Repeat Steps 4 and 5 using the 2½-inch piece of green cord to attach the beard to the center hole in the hat fur.

8 Glue the red nose in place at the top of the beard.

9 Glue more white clay crumbles to the hat fur to cover the green cord knots.

10 Fold the 20-inch green cord in half and loop it through the hole in the top of the hat. Tie the loose ends into a knot. With this hanger, you can now hang Santa in a favorite spot.

Old St. Nick never looked so good or so modern. Enjoy the holidays.

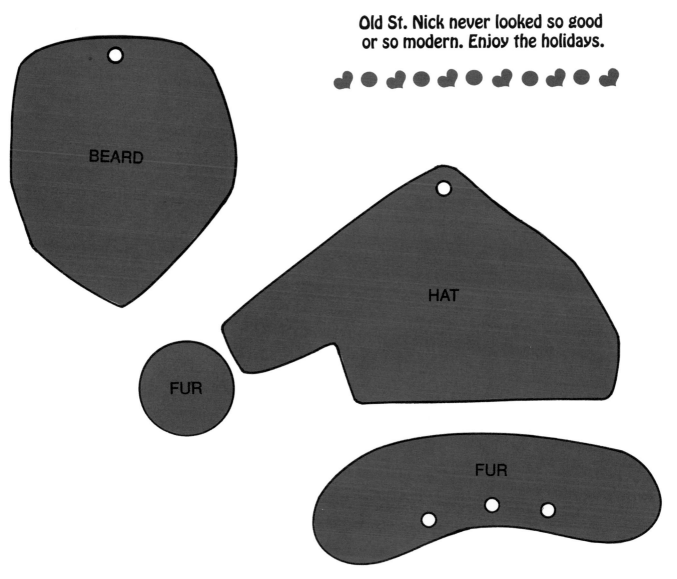

Happy Ho-Ho Man

Santa has a surprise. He totes around a red bag full of magical toys
to bring Christmas wishes to all of your yuletide visitors.

Ask a grown-up to help you purchase some of the check-list items. Also ask a grown-up to help you with the saw and hot glue gun.

CHECK LIST

- ❑ Tracing paper
- ❑ Pencil
- ❑ 10-inch square, 1-inch-thick piece of wood
- ❑ Black felt-tip marker or crayon
- ❑ Wood saw
- ❑ 8-inch-long, 3½-inch-wide, 1-inch-thick piece of wood
- ❑ Acrylic paints: red, white, peach, black, pink, forest green
- ❑ 1-inch-long sponge brushes
- ❑ ½ yard of 1¼-inch-wide white trim
- ❑ 5 yards white polyester cablecord, size 200
- ❑ 1-inch-wide white pom-pom
- ❑ ½ yard of 3-inch-wide red paper twist
- ❑ Cotton ball
- ❑ Hot glue gun and glue sticks
- ❑ Thread

MAKE SANTA

1 Using tracing paper and a pencil, trace the Santa pattern on page 185. Cut out the pattern.

2 Place the pattern on the square piece of wood. Use a marker or crayon to trace around it.

3 Ask a grown-up to help you use a wood saw to cut the Santa shape out.

PAINT & DRESS

1 Use a sponge brush to paint the back and edges of Santa's body red. Let the paint dry.

2 Follow the photograph and draw lines showing the hat, face, and body placement.

3 Paint the hat and body areas red. Look at the photograph.

4 Paint the face peach. Paint 2 black dots for the eyes.

5 Paint the bottom 1¼ inch of the body white. Let the paint dry.

6 Cut the polyester cord into 1 piece, 6-inches long and into 8 pieces, each 1-inch long. Also cut 40 pieces, 4 inches long.

7 Ask a grown-up to help you use the hot glue gun. Glue the 8 small pieces of polyester cord to the forehead for bangs. Unravel about half of the bottom of each piece of cord to make it look like hair.

8 Fold 8 pieces of 4-inch cord in half.

9 Glue 4 pieces at the fold next to the bangs and out to the edge on one side. Glue the other 4 pieces on the other side. Unravel about half of the bottom of each piece to make it look like hair.

10 Fold 30 pieces of 4-inch cord in half.

11 Glue 15 of the pieces at the fold in a line to the bottom part of the face area to form the bottom layer of a beard. Look at the pattern to see what to do.

12 Repeat Step 11, using the other 15 folded pieces of cord to to make the top layer of the beard.

13 Completely unravel the last 2 of the 4-inch pieces and tie a small thread in the middle of each to make tassels.

14 Glue 1 tassel to the top of Santa's hat and glue the other tassel on the face just above the beard to make a mustache.

15 Glue the pom-pom to the top of the hat tassel.

16 Cut the white trim into a 6-inch piece and a 9-inch piece.

17 Glue the smaller piece of white trim across the top of Santa's hair to make a hat cuff. Glue the larger piece over the painted white strip on the bottom.

MAKE STAND & BAG

1 Use a sponge brush to paint the rectangular piece of wood forest green. Let the paint dry.

2 Fold and glue the red paper twist 2 inches on each short end.

3 Fold the red paper twist in half, making the short folded ends meet. Glue at the sides to make a bag.

4 Stuff the bag with cotton. Tie the top of the bag off with the 6-inch piece of polyester cord.

5 Glue the completed Santa and the bag to the painted wood rectangle.

This wood Santa Claus will bring a big holiday smile and brighten any room.

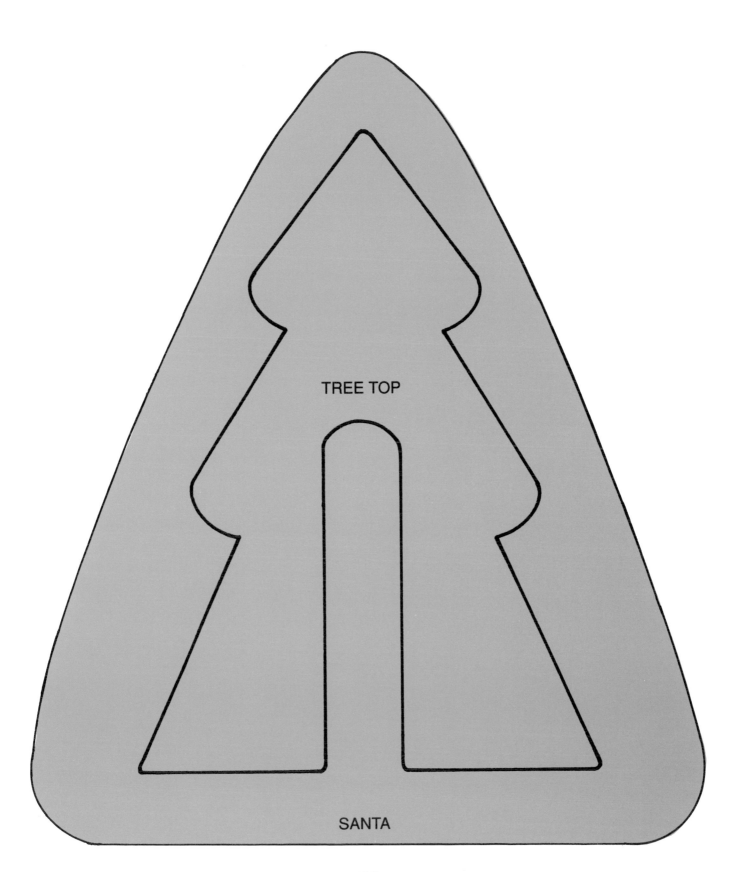

TREE TOP

SANTA

Woodland Tree

Decorate this wood tree with your favorite tiny trinkets. The tree will bring holiday cheer to those who admire the creative work you do.

CHECK LIST

- ❏ Tracing paper
- ❏ Pencil
- ❏ 2 pieces of wood measuring 10-inches by 15-inches by 1-inch
- ❏ Black felt-tip marker or crayon
- ❏ Wood saw
- ❏ Green acrylic paint
- ❏ 1-inch-long sponge brushes
- ❏ Miniature plastic or wood holiday ornaments
- ❏ Hot glue gun and glue sticks

1 Using tracing paper and a pencil, trace the tree patterns on pages 185 and 186. Cut the patterns out.

2 Place the patterns on the wood and trace around them. Ask a grown-up to help you use a saw to cut out the shapes.

3 Using a sponge brush, paint all sides of both tree pieces green. Let the paint dry.

4 Fit top and bottom pieces together. Glue to secure. Glue ornaments to tree.

●●●●●●●●●●●●●●●

This tree can decorate any place in the house and welcome the holiday season.

●●●●●●●●●●●●●●●

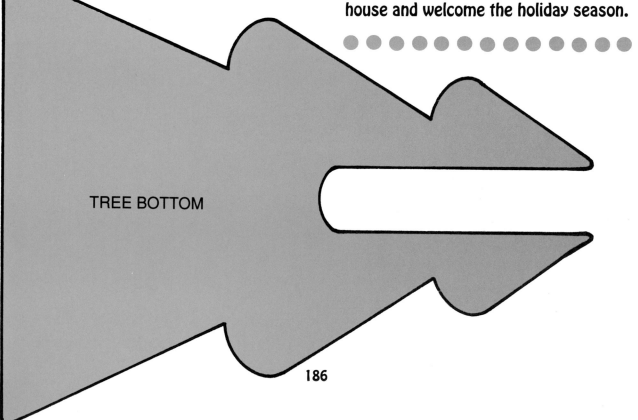

TREE BOTTOM

186

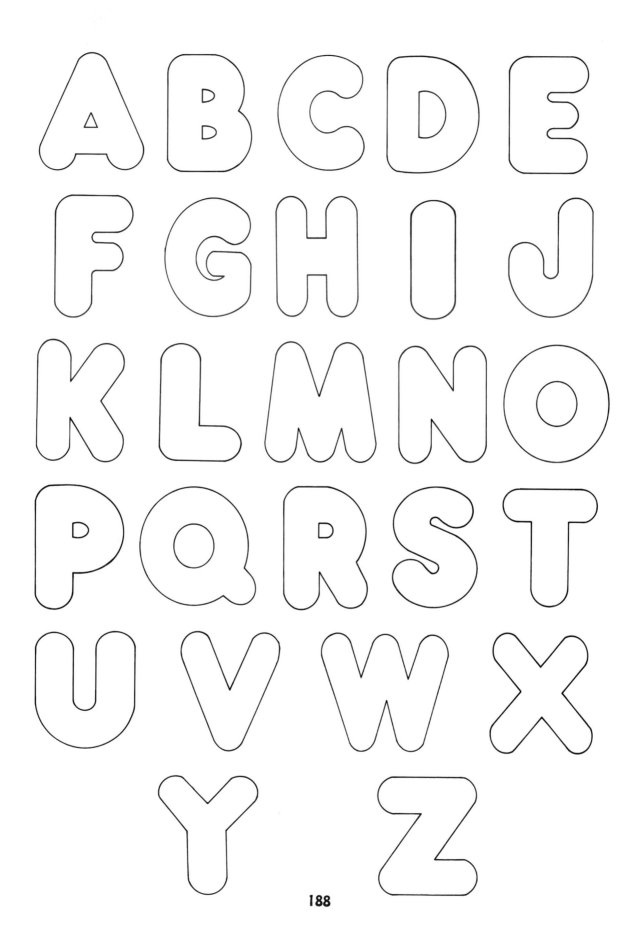

188

General Instructions

✓ CHECK LIST

Read over the items in the Check List for the project you have selected. This list of materials tells you everything you need to purchase or gather to create the project in the photograph.

The number or quantity you will need of these materials also is given. For the most part, the materials and tools you need are listed in the order you use them.

☞ PREPARATION

Gather all the materials and tools in the Check List before you begin. You probably have some of these items in your home. Pencils, tracing paper, scissors, drawing paper, watercolor paints and paintbrushes are among the general supplies you will need. Check with a grown-up in your house to see if you already have some of these items.

You may have to purchase specific items such as ribbon, fabric, acrylic paints, wood, a hot glue gun and glue sticks or a craft knife. You can find these at most arts, crafts, or variety stores.

x SAFETY

When working with an iron, hot glue gun, scissors, knife or spray paints, it is important to be very careful. You may need to ask a grown-up to help you with these tools.

When using spray paints or spray resins, always work outdoors to ensure proper ventilation. Put newspaper down to protect the grass or concrete.

ⓑ PROTECTION

Protect your work table or work area with newspaper, paper towels or aluminum foil. You may find it necessary to put down another layer of cover-up material to protect your project from spilled glue or paints. When painting small items, set them on a larger piece of scratch paper.

Wear a painting smock or an old shirt to protect your clothing from stains. Also, remember to clean up your work area when your craft project is finished.

1 2
3 4 STEP-BY-STEP

Follow the instructions on how to make your project from the first step to the last. The steps give the best order for making the project. Diagrams are included with some instructions to help make the steps clearer. Looking at the photograph of the finished project as you work will also help to make things easy.

The instructions tell you how to most closely match the project in the photograph. But the best part about creating something yourself is that you are unique. Craft the project in your own way. Use your imagination and don't hesitate to make changes.

👫 SKILL LEVELS

We do not list an age or skill level for the craft projects in the book. You should simply choose the ones you want to make. Let your interests, imagination and abilities determine the projects you create. As you continue to have fun with crafts and become successful with your first few endeavors, you will build the confidence and skill needed to complete those projects that seem more difficult.

✏ MAKING PATTERNS

Making patterns is fun and easy. Your first step is to trace the pattern from the book. Place your tracing paper over the pattern and trace it with a pencil.

If the pattern is a large or medium shape, cut out your traced pattern. Set the cutout pattern on your project material or paper. Then, draw around the shape.

If the pattern is a face or something more detailed, tape a piece of carbon paper on your project material or paper. Make sure the carbon side is against the project material. Tape your traced pattern on top of the carbon paper and draw over the

pattern again. The carbon will transfer your pattern to the project material or paper. Be careful not to press too hard, though. You don't want carbon smudges on your project.

You can also use an embroidery transfer pencil to make pattern details on your project. It is like carbon paper in a pencil. Use it to trace the pattern from the book, then turn the tracing over and rub over the lines to transfer them to your project. The image will be reversed.

If the pattern should be cut from fabric, pin your traced pattern onto the fabric and simply cut around it. Repeat this step to cut as many of each piece as the instructions indicate.

✂ CUTTING STENCILS

To make a stencil, cut out your traced pattern and draw around it on a manila folder with a pencil. Or, transfer the pattern to the folder using carbon paper. Trace 1 stencil for each color used in the design. Draw a square 1-inch-wide border around each design.

You may need to ask a grown-up to help you cut around the stencil pattern with a craft knife as described in the project instructions. Then, with scissors, cut the stencil out of the folder by following the 1-inch border lines.

Tape the stencil to your project material and follow the instructions for brush or sponge painting.

🖌 PAINTING

You can practice painting, dry-brush painting and sponge painting on a piece of art paper before you start your project so that you know what look you want.

DRY-BRUSH PAINTING

In dry-brush painting, you pick up a small amount of thick color on a brush that has not been dipped in water. Move the brush lightly over a dry painting surface. The paint will catch on the raised bumps of the craft material or paper, leaving tiny speckles of paint and letting the background paint or surface show through. This step is often used to show the texture of a weathered or worn surface.

SPONGE PAINTING

Painting with a sponge will also give your project texture. The sponge makes dot-like patterns with the paint while a paintbrush makes lines. You can paint with a dry or wet sponge. You can also press a damp sponge into wet paint already on your paper to lift out color and leave texture in its place.

☼ DRAWING CIRCLES

One of the easiest ways to draw a circle is to use a compass and pencil. To draw a 4-inch-wide circle, set the compass at 2 inches, put the needle in the spot where you want the middle of the circle, press the pencil to the paper or project and turn the compass around to draw the circle. Always set the compass at half the width you want the finished circle.

Another way to draw a circle is to trace around something round. Choose a drinking glass, a bowl, or any other round container. To make sure you get the size of circle you want, measure the width of the round item with a ruler. Place the item on your paper or project and trace around it with a pencil, crayon, or marker.

〜 TRANSFER WEB

Some of the projects call for iron-on, paper-backed transfer web. This is a material that when ironed between two pieces of fabric, fuses them together. In some projects you will use transfer web to stick one color material to another color. In other projects, a piece of fabric is strengthened by using transfer web to fuse it to another piece and double the thickness of the fabric.

In both cases, ask a grown-up to help you position and iron the transfer web to the fabric. The transfer web has one rough glue side and one smooth paper side. Place the rough side against the wrong side of the fabric. Iron on the paper side to fuse the transfer web to the fabric. Remove the paper. Position fabric with the transfer-web side down on a second piece of fabric. Iron over the fabric to fuse the two together.

Index

All of us at Meredith® Press are dedicated to offering you, our customer, the best books we can create. We are particularly concerned that all of the instructions for making projects are clear and accurate. Please address your correspondence to Customer Service Department, Meredith® Press, Meredith® Corporation, 150 East 52nd Street, New York, NY 10022 or call 1-800-678-2665.